Futures & Options

Donald Spence

Futures & Options

Donald Spence

Glenlake Publishing Company, Ltd.

Chicago • London • New Delhi

AMACOM

American Management Association

New York • Atlanta • Boston • Chicago • Kansas City • San Francisco • Washington, D.C.
Brussels • Mexico City • Tokyo • Toronto

This book is available at a special
discount when ordered in bulk quantities.
For information, contact Special Sales Department,
AMACOM, an imprint of AMA Publications, a division of
American Management Association,
1601 Broadway, New York, NY 10019.

332.644
F996

© 1999 Woodhead Publishing Ltd.

ISBN: 0-8144-0507-X

Printing number

10 9 8 7 6 5 4 3 2 1

Contents

Foreword   *ix*

Introduction   *xi*

Contributors   *xiv*

Part 1: Markets, instruments and trading   **1**

1   History of the markets   3
Early days *3*   Development of futures and options markets *4*
Derivatives *6*   Recent developments *8*

2   The 24-hour market   9
Globex *9*   Access *11*   Project A *11*
Advantages and disadvantages of electronic trading *11*

3   The exchanges and their contracts   14
The London International Financial Futures Exchange (LIFFE) *14*
The International Petroleum Exchange (IPE) *18*
The London Metal Exchange (LME) *19*
The London Bullion Market Association (LBMA) *22*
The London Securities and Derivatives Exchange (OMLX) *23*
The Chicago Board of Trade (CBOT) *24*
The Mid America Commodity Exchange (MIDAM) *25*
The Chicago Mercantile Exchange (CME) *25*
The Chicago Board Options Exchange (CBOE) *26*

The New York Mercantile Exchange (NYMEX) *27*
The Coffee, Sugar and Cocoa Exchange (CSCE) *28*
The New York Cotton Exchange (NYCE) *29*
The Philadelphia Stock Exchange (PHLX) *30*
The Kansas City Board of Trade (KCBOT) *30*
The Minneapolis Grain Exchange (MGE) *30*
Marché à Terme International de France (MATIF) *31*
Deutsche Terminbörse (DTB) *32*
Other European exchanges *32*   The Winnipeg Commodity
Exchange (WCE) *33*   Other Canadian exchanges *33*
Bolsa de Mercadorias & Futuros (BM&F) *34*
The Sydney Futures Exchange (SFE) *35*
The New Zealand Futures and Options Exchange (NZFOE) *35*
Japanese futures exchanges *35*   The Singapore International
Monetary Exchange (SIMEX) *37*   The Hong Kong Futures
Exchange (HKFE) *38*   Other Far Eastern exchanges *38*
China *39*   The former Soviet Union and Eastern Europe *39*
South Africa *40*

4

Using exchange-traded futures and options   41
Hedging *42*   Arbitrage *45*   Spreading *46*
Trading systems *46*   Clearing *47*   Market analysis *47*
Options *49*   Funds *52*

5

OTC derivatives   54
OTC interest rate and foreign exchange products *54*   Swaps *55*
OTC options *59*   Other OTC derivatives *61*
Uses of OTC derivatives *62*   Market participants *65*
Market size *66*   Risk management of OTC derivatives *67*
Conclusion *68*

6

Managed futures   70
Background *70*   Market observations *72*
Results support theory *73*   The professional managers *74*
Trading styles *74*   The Commodity Pool
Operator (CPO or manager of managers) *76*
Managed futures information *76*
Managed futures terminology *77*   Remuneration *77*
Structures *78*   The guaranteed fund *79*
Measuring returns *80*

7 Market analysis 82
The Elliott Wave and Quantum theories *83*
Candlesticks *84* Other technical indicators *85*
Neural networks *86* Exotic options *87*
Fundamental analysis *87*

Part 2: Regulation and management **91**

8 Lessons from the past 93
Examples of fraudulent trading *94* The tin crisis *95*
Recent events *96* Market manipulation *97*
Cold-calling *100* Conclusion *101*

9 Regulation and compliance 102
The European Union *104* UK regulation *105*
The United States of America *114*

10 Training and education 117
Registered Representative examination *118*
Exchange training programmes for floor traders *120*
Additional courses and training *121*

11 The taxation of futures and options 123
United Kingdom *123* Europe *129*
United States of America *133* Conclusion *134*

Part 3: The future **135**

12 The way ahead 137
Market transparency *138* European Monetary Union (EMU) *139*
Inter-exchange links *140* Exchange-traded versus OTC
products *142* Smaller contracts *142* Education, regulation
and clearing *142*

13 Future futures 144
Insurance futures *144* Property futures *145* New energy
futures *146* New metals futures *146* New agricultural
futures *147* New financial futures *147* Conclusion *148*

Appendix A
Contract specifications *149*

Appendix B
Exchange addresses *181*

Appendix C
Glossary of terms *186*

Appendix D
Abbreviations *194*

Appendix E
Some exotic options *197*

Index 201

Foreword

The primary role of derivatives is to facilitate the transfer of risk – not to create it – and the vast majority of corporate and other market users use these instruments prudently and successfully for this very purpose. Even so, the recent worldwide proliferation in futures and options exchanges, products and customers has created a need for better understanding of market and trading practice, procedure and regulation. Moreover, the importance of having adequate product knowledge (as well as effective internal controls and procedures) has been more than demonstrated by a number of recent well-publicised losses incurred by corporate and institutional users of the markets. Indeed, nearly all the recently published guidelines on managing derivatives risk have emphasised that, while it may not be necessary for Boards of Directors to have a detailed understanding of particular derivative products, they must be sufficiently knowledgeable to formulate and agree corporate policy for their use.

For those who wish to acquire the necessary basic understanding, this book provides an excellent introduction and overview of markets and industry practice and should help to dispel much of the mystique surrounding the world of 'derivatives'.

Anthony Belchambers
Chief Executive Officer
The Futures and Options Association

Introduction

Futures and options, under the guise of that all-embracing buzzword derivatives, have received a mixed press in recent years, but there is no excuse for ignorance of derivative markets. The language may seem strange at first but there is nothing mysterious about them. However, aided by the collapse of Baring Brothers in 1995, several high profile and spectacular transgressions by both management and staff have combined to give the industry a bad name in the eyes of outsiders. Nevertheless, there is no getting away from the fact that derivatives have transformed financial markets; it is now possible to avoid almost any risk of adverse market movements by the judicious use of them. Not all participants use them for that purpose, however, preferring to go for the huge profits that could accrue through speculation. For every winner, though, there has to be a loser and such profits can quickly dissolve into equally huge losses.

Speculation is an integral part of futures and options trading; without the speculator, the markets could not exist. Indeed, the whole concept of futures trading is that the speculator takes the risk to enable the trade to hedge their operations. To many, futures and options remain an esoteric business, beyond the comprehension of ordinary mortals. Such is very far from the case; the majority of them are not in any sense complex. They are derivative products based on the performance of the underlying financial instrument whether it be a bond, commodity, share or an interest or currency rate. Futures and options are the simplest kind of derivatives. Futures are agreements to buy or sell particular assets at an agreed future date and price. Options agreements give the buyer the right, but not the obligation, to do so. As risk management tools they are second to none; the fact that companies can use derivatives in this way has led to a dramatic increase in their use. Some American companies have even been sued for not using them.

There is no reason why ignorance of these extremely useful tools should preclude anyone from using them to their own advantage and it is hoped that this book will go a long way towards explaining how they work. It is aimed at all levels of experience of derivatives from the student contemplating a career in the financial world to managers whose task it is to supervise traders and whose lack of expertise has sometimes proved instrumental in allowing several rogue traders to operate undetected for far too long. The need for education of all in the industry, including those only on the periphery, is of paramount importance. By no means all transgressors are fraudsters; ignorance played all too prominent a part in many of the cases that have hit the headlines recently and the potential rewards available from successful operations tend to cloud the judgement of impetuous traders and blind them to the pitfalls. The desire to stand out amongst one's fellow workers is very strong and can lead to rash decisions; it is dangerous to allow traders to operate unchecked.

The industry is now truly a global one with continuous trading going on around the clock; it is an industry that never sleeps. Exchange link-ups across time zones are multiplying and mutual offset agreements are set to increase, making such trading easier and cheaper.

Derivatives are traded both on- and off-exchange with the former method far more transparent than the other. Indeed off-exchange trading, also known as over-the-counter (OTC) trading, is often accused of excessive secrecy and is also largely unregulated. They are mostly individually tailored contracts invented for specific purposes with the investor, or grantor, taking the other side of the contract and, by extension, all the risk inherent in it. They are usually between banks or other financial institutions and large corporate organisations.

It is the lack of transparency of these contracts that has led to criticisms of secrecy and the unregulated nature of the market that has led to efforts by exchanges to offer contracts that could attract business away from OTC markets. Contracts like Brady bonds and yield curve spread options have consequently appeared to try and achieve this but have so far had only limited effect.

US exchanges, in particular, are introducing futures and options on smaller currencies to try and replace those that will be lost after European Monetary Union (EMU). The proliferation of new contracts has made us very aware of how difficult it is to keep up to date with events. Consequently, there will, unfortunately, be errors and omissions in Appendix A as new contracts get regulatory approval and start trading.

Co-operation between exchanges is proceeding apace and many link-ups have already been established. Many more will happen, particularly in Europe where, in the run-up to EMU, there will be many changes and, inevitably, closures. At present, there are many small exchanges in almost every European country and it will be impossible for all of them to become international. Indeed, many will be destined to offer only domestic contracts to domestic customers. It looks likely that the currency markets are in for a dramatic upheaval from 1999, as many old European favourites disappear to be replaced by an untested Euro to compete with the world's currencies.

Regulation remains an enigma; just how to pitch it continues to occupy the minds of regulators. Too much regulation will drive the business underground and too little will produce more rogue traders and angry shareholders. However, there is always a need to tighten up supervision and, unfortunately, the industry does not appear willing to do so voluntarily. Excessive governmental interference is not helpful but self-regulation is scarcely an option nowadays with such huge amounts of money at stake. The situation is constantly under review and an acceptable balance must eventually be found. The abolition of the Commodity Futures Trading Commission (CFTC) of the US, threatened by the Senate would seem a retrograde step; NYMEX's (New York Merchantile Exchange) boast that a scandal of the magnitude of the Sumitomo copper debacle could not happen there is belied by the fact that it supports deregulation of futures and options exchanges.

It has been said that derivatives are not the problem – people are, but the fact remains that the industry reveals its secrets and intricacies only reluctantly and the purpose of this book is to lift the lid a little further to prove that futures and options are just another existing market offering tremendous rewards to anyone interested enough to learn the basics.

Contributors

Nicholas Burge is Head of Swaps at Nomura International in London (Ch 5).
The Futures & Options Association is the trade association for the futures and options industry (Ch 9 & 10).
Victor Levy is a Tax Partner at Arthur Andersen, London (Ch 11). Arthur Andersen is authorised by the Institute of Chartered Accountants in England and Wales to carry on investment business.
Ian Morley is a director of John Govett & Co, London (Ch 6).
Donald Spence is an author and journalist, writing extensively on the derivatives markets (Ch 1, 2, 3, 4, 7, 8, 12 & 13).

Markets, instruments and trading

1

History of the markets

Early days

Today's huge futures and options industry owes its existence to the early commodity trading and money-changing activities that can be traced back to Roman times. At that time, every town had its market and the area around the Tower of London was a veritable hive of activity. Flemish traders in the 12th century are credited with being the first to use forward contracts. In London, activity moved to the Royal Exchange in 1571 after it was opened by Queen Elizabeth I and it quickly became a popular meeting place and the forerunner for many of today's exchanges.

The Royal Exchange was destroyed in the Great Fire of 1666 and, while it was being rebuilt, traders operated from the numerous coffee houses that abounded in the City. In order that their customers would know where to find them, each trader frequented the same coffee house every day. Trading from these coffee houses became so popular that few moved back to the Royal Exchange.

After another serious fire in 1748, commodity traders set up shop at Garroways coffee house, which had one floor reserved for auctions. Trading continued there until 1860 when it was demolished. In the meantime, the London Commercial Salerooms had opened in Mincing Lane in 1811 and activities gradually relocated there. Merchants and brokers were initially reluctant to move there, however, as the general depression arising from the Napoleonic wars restricted trade. However, things started to improve in the 1830s, and by 1880 it was flourishing. Its success continued until the building was destroyed by bombs in 1941.

In the meantime, futures and options trading had begun and, by the outbreak of the Second World War, was flourishing, albeit in a very unsophisticated way compared with today's activity. Options had first been traded in Amsterdam in the 17th century although, for many years, pricing them was pure guesswork.

Development of futures and options markets

The first futures markets were opened in Chicago around the middle of the 19th century, to trade the main agricultural products: wheat, maize (corn) and soyabeans. The need for them arose from a desire on the part of farmers for an efficient and reliable method of hedging and financing their production, following some serious defaults in previous years on forward contracts by unscrupulous operators. The markets soon attracted the speculators who greatly aided their development by broadening and deepening them in the search for excitement and profit.

The present Chicago futures markets, the Chicago Board of Trade (CBOT) and the Chicago Mercantile Exchange (CME), are the largest in the world. These Exchanges are fully diversified and now provide many contracts that are far removed from their origins; from them, grew the whole futures trading industry.

Futures markets evolved from the shortcomings of forward trading; the need constantly to have the backing of the physical commodity became too much of a financial burden for many producers. End-users, too, had problems with storing and insurance in what was often a very volatile market. Counterparty risk was also a major worry: unscrupulous operators thought nothing of walking away from their obligations if the markets turned against them. In a spot market, there is no risk because the entire transaction is completed in one go; forward markets, on the other hand, can have a long lead time, all the while at the mercy of fluctuating prices.

Futures markets were the solution to these problems, providing a mechanism that supplied forward prices to reduce the risks of volatile spot markets and which were free of counterparty risk. A futures market has two important features that forward markets do not have: first, they have standardised quality requirements, delivery locations and arbitration procedures and, second, the counterparty risk is negated by the establishment of a clearing house which guarantees that the contract will be honoured even in the event of a default by one party to it. Once the contract has been agreed on the floor or pit of a futures exchange, it becomes two contracts, each with the clearing house acting as counterparty. The seller has in fact sold to the clearing house and the buyer has bought from it. The net position, however, remains the same – the seller still has the obligation to sell and the buyer to buy.

Nevertheless, in order to do this with any degree of confidence, it is necessary to be certain of the integrity of the participants. Membership of the exchanges, therefore, is carefully vetted and companies are nowadays required to provide a substantial capital base to be accepted. This has to be constantly topped up in the event of an increase in trading commitments. In addition, customers' accounts must be strictly segregated from in-house ones.

During the second half of the 19th century, the growth of futures markets in North America and Europe accelerated once the concept had been firmly established. A sugar futures market opened in Hamburg in 1880 and a coffee market in New York two years later.

Futures trading in Europe ceased altogether during the First World War and the Americans were quick to take advantage of the situation; the New York Coffee Exchange launched a sugar contract in 1916 and consequently changed its name to the New York Coffee and Sugar Exchange. Cocoa was added in 1979 following a merger with the cocoa exchange that had been founded in 1925.

London's first 'soft' futures market was a sugar one; founded in 1888, it was for raw beet, fob Hamburg. When it reopened after the First World War, it became a white sugar contract and this lasted until 1931. In 1929, however, tariff changes had virtually stopped the import of refined sugar, so another, different, raw contract was required and subsequently launched in 1931.

The London Metal Exchange (LME) was established in 1877, trading copper and tin. The market hours were quickly set and the tradition of short, sharp 'ring' trading established. Three months was regarded as the ideal date for forward contracts as this was the approximate sailing time from Santiago and Singapore to the UK, for Chilean bars and Straits tin, respectively. Lead, zinc and pig-iron were also traded but in separate groups and subsidiary rings.

It was not until after the Second World War that the industry came to resemble that which we know today. First, in 1971, gold became freely tradable as the US authorities effectively severed the link between currencies and gold, converting the latter from legal currency into a financial asset. The carefully structured system of monetary stability, gold standards and disciplined currencies had been changed for ever.

It was not long before currencies themselves became a target for reform, and futures and options trading in financial instruments opened on the fledgling International Monetary Market (now part of the CME) in Chicago in 1972. The first financial futures were currency contracts and these were followed, in 1977, by the three-month Treasury bill futures contract. Interest rate futures were introduced in 1986. The London International Financial Futures Exchange (LIFFE) opened in 1982. The growth of financial futures trading was phenomenal; it achieved in 15 years what other markets took over a century to do. This was due mainly to the tremendous advances in telecommunications which attracted more money and more people to the markets in a very short space of time. Nowadays, marketing and publicity given to the launch of new contracts are also far more sophisticated.

The evolution of the different markets is described in later chapters. Since around 1985, literally hundreds of contracts, covering everything from cheddar cheese to recyclable goods and from catastrophe insurance to natural gas, have been launched. Many of them did not stand the test of time and were quickly de-listed. However, if the same standards in use today were applied in the 1950s and 1960s, we would have far fewer contracts, as in those days the exchange authorities were far more tolerant of a new contract and prepared to allow an even longer period for it to become established.

Nevertheless, all major – and many minor – trading centres now have their own financial futures markets and cross-border co-operation, mutual offsetting and 24-hour trading agreements are on the increase.

The traditional method of trading futures was by open outcry, whereby all trading members congregated on one place and shouted their needs for all to hear. Nowadays, that method is becoming rarer, as traders prefer to remain in their offices, trading from screens. The face-to-face confrontation that is open outcry trading provided much more scope for speculation and could even engineer the short-term manipulation of prices in order to attempt to trigger a particular chart point that would generate extra business. Open outcry also means that all participants trade on a level playing-field, with all market-sensitive news available to everyone. While screen-based trading is cheaper and easier to set up, open outcry brings narrower spreads, faster execution and greater liquidity – the last being the most vital. Fortunately, not all exchanges have switched to the electronic system and open outcry is still stoutly defended in some quarters. There is little doubt that the latter system adds more value for the user.

Derivatives

From the proliferation of new financial contracts grew interest rate and several different index contracts, all of which began to attract a different kind of user. The objectives of futures trading include the containment of price risk and the reduction of operating costs; simple hedging strategies had, hitherto, sufficed. But the emergence of this new type of user – led by the fund manager – changed the entire complexion of the markets and led to the dominance of the so-called derivatives markets.

These derivatives markets are no different from the futures and options markets of former years; it is just that an alternative name seems to add importance to what is, in effect, a very simple operation. For instance, options are derivatives of futures, while futures are themselves derivatives of physicals. The growth of futures and options funds added a new dimension to the markets as more and more money was pumped into them by people who neither knew (nor cared) about the underlying instrument. They were simply following their own trading theories, often based on chart patterns that traced past movements and from which they hoped to be able to predict future movements. This inevitably distorted prices in the short term, sometimes making it difficult for genuine trade operations to undertake their hedging strategies.

The situation was exacerbated by the advent of the hedge funds, comprising huge amounts of money boosted by leveraged borrowings. In 1993/4, these unregulated investment vehicles were seen at one point as a threat to the very fabric of the world's financial system as they trawled the markets in search of a quick profit. Fortunately, the realities of the marketplace have caused a change of direction. The hedge funds became too big and their managers soon realised that they were unable to operate effectively in such large amounts: taking a position distorted prices one way and getting out had the same effect the other way. The result was a sharply reduced profit and, sometimes, a quite unnecessary loss. Hedge funds consequently broke up into several, non-specialised, smaller ones, giving managers better scope to operate. The trend towards smaller funds is now well established, but, as their numbers increase, price distortions seem likely to continue.

The futures and options markets have, from time to time, been the victims of some bad publicity and unwarranted attention. When that happens, calls for yet more regulation and curbs grow louder. Such calls come usually from the media and government agencies, neither of which perhaps properly understands the workings of the markets. One of the most celebrated causes of recent bad publicity was the activities of Mr Nick Leeson and the fall of Barings Bank. Fears of total disruption of the markets and the threat of systemic risk were very real at that time, and it is reassuring that such calamities were avoided. The speed and efficiency of the authorities, in particular the Singapore International Monetary Exchange (SIMEX), to offset and close out any open contracts were very impressive. The implications of this episode are discussed in a later chapter.

Recent developments

Significant changes took place in the 1990s. The most important of these was the escalation of inter-exchange co-operation across time zones. Pioneered by the CME and SIMEX in 1984, it had become widespread by 1996, with no exchange wanting to be left out.

Inter-exchange co-operation takes the form of mutual offsetting of contracts in both exchanges, permitting a member or customer of either exchange to transfer a position executed on one exchange to the clearing house of the other exchange. Following the successful CME/SIMEX agreement, which was renewed in 1994, the following tie-ups have been or are being set up: LIFFE/CBOT, LIFFE/TIFFE, MATIF/DTB, PHLX/HKFE, LIFFE/MEFF. This list is far from comprehensive and there will be others in time.

Exchange mergers are also taking place with increasing frequency. Talks between the London Commodity Exchange (LCE) and LIFFE and between CBOT and CME have reached advanced stages with the first two merging in September 1996, and more will follow. European Union directives easing cross-border trading in Europe will lead to more mergers and the likely demise of some of the smaller exchanges. All this is more widely discussed in another chapter.

Information sharing is also on the increase. At Boca Raton in Florida, USA, in March 1996, 49 futures exchanges signed an agreement to improve and refine techniques for this purpose, to strengthen the financial integrity of exchange-traded markets.

2

The 24-hour market

The fantastic growth of derivatives markets in the late 1980s and early 1990s created a need for investors to transcend time zones to enable them to trade around the clock. This need was fulfilled by the invention of Globex, the world's first 24-hour electronic trading system. Globex was developed by Reuters for the two main Chicago exchanges, Chicago Board of Trade (CBOT) andChicago Mercantile Exchange (CME). Hailed as the dawn of a new era by its three main shareholders, Globex was launched in 1992. The fear that other exchanges in different time zones might try and duplicate Chicago's most successful contracts gave the scheme added impetus. Since derivatives cannot be patented, longer trading hours seemed a logical extension for the expansion of business.

Globex

Globex is a worldwide electronic trade-matching system of futures and options orders for use after the close of a participating exchange's open outcry trading hours. It is accessible around the world and enables trading to take place around the clock. By using Globex, investors no longer have to await the opening of an exchange to adjust their positions to take account of overnight events in other financial centres.

Trading on Globex was initially confined to currencies and bonds, but interest rates and equity instruments were soon added. The first contracts to be traded were the CME's currencies and the CBOT's ten-year Treasury Note futures; they quickly expanded to include Eurodollars and Treasury Bonds. The only non-US participating exchange at this stage was the Marché à Terme International de France (MATIF), whose Pibor, Notional Bond and Ecu Bond contracts were linked into the system by the beginning of 1993.

Expansion of the system to other exchanges was hampered by disagreements as to which contracts would or could not be allowed to be traded. For instance, the CME refused to allow LIFFE's successful Eurodollar contract to compete in direct competition with its own, with the result that LIFFE refused to join it.

Notwithstanding further expansion in Hong Kong and Geneva in the first half of 1993 and approval to trade in Japan, overall reactions to the system were not encouraging. This was reflected in volumes which, by this time, were averaging a total of only 3000 lots per day on 300 screens worldwide. Volumes were boosted significantly when the MATIF contracts began trading in March 1993, posting a record 14 292 lots on the 19th of that month.

LIFFE's refusal to join was a serious setback to the system's viability; however, it was CBOT's refusal to allow LIFFE's German Bund contract to be added to the list and the announcement that CBOT would even launch its own Bund contract which served to demonstrate that the dominance and protectionism of the two Chicago exchanges had begun to form a serious obstacle to other exchanges joining the system. The perception that membership of Globex would give control of the Chicago exchanges' products to their rivals was very strong. The issue of exclusivity – that only one instrument based on one underlying product can be listed – was considered by the two exchanges as central to the Globex philosophy and necessary to maximise the liquidity of any contract on the system. Many non-US exchange officials did not see it that way; why should rival contracts, which compete daily in the futures pits, not do the same on Globex?

In order to save the whole concept, therefore, ways had to be found to rekindle interest in the system. However, any attempts at restructuring and relaxing of the rules failed to bring this about; the two Chicago exchanges simply could not agree on a way forward. By April 1994, CBOT had had enough and opted out of the system. In truth, the world had moved on from electronic 24-hour trading towards more inter-exchange co-operation, and negotiations along those lines had already started.

Only MATIF had taken significant advantage of Globex and, by the end of 1993, it accounted for 87% of its volume. MATIF had scrapped its own successful after-hours trading system on joining Globex. However, the future of Globex was called into question by MATIF's decision to pull out when its contract expires in April 1998. MATIF intends to adopt the Bourse's Nouveau Systeme de Cotation (NSC).

Access

NYMEX's (New York Mercantile Exchange) Access system, another after-hours electronic trading system, started a year earlier than Globex. A rather low-key affair, from its outset it was rather less ambitious. It was consequently rather more successful. Confined to NYMEX's own – mainly energy – contracts and initially to US investors, volumes quickly exceeded targets. In November 1993, it opened its system in London. Though on a much smaller scale than Globex, volumes were not far short of the two Chicago exchanges combined. Access has significant advantages over Globex: its energy contracts are genuinely global, whereas many of Chicago's financial products are not traded widely in Europe or the Far East. The futures market has an important role to play in oil; the underlying cash market is often opaque (unlike currencies). Turnover in 1996 was 2.5 million lots, compared with 0.5 million in 1995.

Project A

Having opted out of Globex, CBOT created its own after-hours trading system, Project A. Launched in October 1994, it opened initially for only two hours in the afternoon, bridging the gap between the close of CBOT's afternoon session and the opening of its evening session. Plans to extend trading through the night commenced in November 1995. Trading on Project A is limited to CBOT members. Plans to offer access to the system on Bloomburg terminals worldwide are under discussion but, at present, most of the terminals are in Chicago with a few in New York.

LIFFE has a similar system, APT (Automated Pit Trading System), allowing trading from offices during the evenings when US markets are still trading. It also has an electronic options trading system, APT plus, which allows members to trade German Government Bond (Bund) options from their own offices for 25 minutes after floor trading ceases, complementing the trading of Bund futures during the APT evening session.

Advantages and disadvantages of electronic trading

Twenty-four-hour electronic trading systems have failed to win the volume of trades that their architects expected. This is partly because it took so long for such electronic trading to get going; plans were first set in motion in 1986 but it was not until 1992 that trading started. Now, things have moved on towards the linking-up of floor-traded exchanges to allow investors access to markets in different time zones. In 1995, LIFFE and

CBOT announced a deal which allows them to trade each other's most popular contracts during the other's opening hours after their own exchanges are closed, and many similar deals have been finalised since then.

This also cuts down on the amount of electronic trading. Many predicted that floor traders and open outcry trading would quickly disappear with the advance of electronic technology. That, however, has not happened and the latter method of trading was still proving extremely resilient in 1996. There are two reasons for this: first, the floor traders themselves are bent on preserving their jobs and, second, the technological advances that were expected to have supplanted them cannot yet reproduce all the qualities that floor traders bring to their markets. Recent developments indicate that support for the open outcry method will continue to be encouraged, as it will always have significant advantages over screen-trading. Many exchanges are investing heavily in new property to accommodate more traders and back-up staff on bigger trading floors.

Many smaller exchanges, however, are entirely electronically traded and these do not enjoy the liquidity of the open outcry method. Moves to shift more contracts from exchanges using the latter towards electronic systems have been slow to catch on and have met resistance. For instance, co-operation between MATIF and Deutsche Terminbörse (DTB), the German electronic exchange, has met with problems as traders have objected to a plan to transfer a popular contract from the floor of MATIF onto screens as part of the ambitious link-up between the two markets.

LIFFE thought it would be possible to improve trading by performing many tasks electronically, but soon discovered that the existing system is capable of handling an order into a pit and out again in less than three seconds. Open outcry trading, however, is not cost-effective and, unless a contract is incredibly busy and turnover is huge, costs are a worry. Concerns about costs are increasing because of a decline in turnover at some exchanges. After years of rapid growth, for example, 1995 was a disappointing year.

Cost, efficiency and regulation are all considerations that need to be taken into account. Traders might prefer the floor-based system but the regulatory authorities prefer the screen-based system where there is far greater transparency. Floor trading, however, has important advantages over electronic systems; it is more liquid and more secure. It is quicker and easier for customers to enter and exit a market, and it is easier to place large orders for institutional clients. The greater transparency of electronic systems works against that. Large buy or sell orders are immediately visible on the screens and this can work against a client's interest. On a trading floor, these large orders can be broken up into smaller ones or otherwise disguised to enable the client to operate in relative secrecy. A further point in open outcry's favour is the rapid advance in technology – the speed of it is so quick that systems soon become outdated. Moreover, it seems that even the most sophisticated electronic systems are too inflexible to handle some of the most complicated trades. Computers still trail far behind the power of the human brain in many areas.

Nevertheless, electronic systems have their place; out-of-hours trading is clearly not possible any other way and it is untrue to say that none of them is as liquid as a floor-based system. Three of Europe's largest exchanges, DTB, OM Stockholm (OM) and Swiss Options and Financial Futures Exchange (SOFFEX), provide some of the world's busiest and most liquid contracts. The real advantage of screen-based systems is their ability to expand across borders and into different time zones. Even those exchanges that rigorously defend the open outcry system – CME, CBOT, LIFFE, MATIF and NYMEX – have all introduced their own electronic systems for just that purpose. It remains to be seen if investors will continue to need a 24-hour trading system or whether they will prefer mutual offsetting opportunities. The original purpose of electronic systems – to provide an after-hours trading vehicle – has changed. However, they also provide a cheap method of launching less liquid, non-core products, allowing a wider range of participants to gain access to the exchanges. The more people that can be attracted to the markets in this way, the better. LIFFE's own after-hours system, APT, is often used as a vehicle for new contracts.

CBOT's Project A and NYMEX's Access are also both used as a means of trading new, illiquid contracts in addition to their after-hours activity. These new contracts are traded within normal trading hours and are not usually tradable after hours. Both are now open during open outcry trading hours for that purpose. Contracts currently being so traded include stainless steel, non-ferrous scrap, jet fuel and coal.

Following Access's successful foray into London, a further link-up with the Sydney Futures Exchange (SFE) has been agreed and negotiations are well advanced with Singapore International Monetary Exchange (SIMEX). Meanwhile SIMEX has a very successful mutual offset arrangement with CME which has been in place for a number of years.

Twenty-four-hour trading systems have not been an unqualified success; interest has not been as high as hoped and volumes are low. Dealing spreads are, understandably, very wide, reflecting the level of interest, and executions, as a result, are often unsatisfactory. All this has led to a change of direction on the part of the exchanges; trends now are more towards link-ups, mutual offsets and trading each other's best contracts in different time zones. This is discussed in greater detail in another chapter.

The tussle between screen and floor trading continues; at present, both have a part to play. However, once the technology has advanced far enough to be able to compete with the human brain, screen trading will probably win the battle. After all, neural networks – trading systems that replicate human thought – are far advanced and actively worked on by many technical traders.

CHAPTER

3

The exchanges and their contracts

The London International Financial Futures Exchange (LIFFE)

LIFFE was founded in 1982, following the phenomenal growth of financial futures trading in the United States since its inception in 1972. By 1985, London and Chicago accounted for half the total of all futures trading in Britain and America. The reason for this extraordinary growth was the exceptional volatility in inflation, interest rates and exchange rates since the collapse of the Bretton Woods Agreement in 1971.

Although the newest of London's exchanges, LIFFE's success has been spectacular and, since its inception, it has grown steadily to become the leading futures and options exchange in Europe and the third largest in the world. It trades in a wide range of fixed income and interest rate products in most of the world's major currencies. Following its merger, in 1992, with the London Traded Options Market, it also provides options on 72 UK equities as well as futures and options on the FTSE 100 and mid-250 indices.

At the end of 1991, LIFFE moved to new, purpose-built premises at Cannonbridge but growth has continued at such a rate since then that these are proving inadequate. Consequently, arrangements have been made to lease the former London Stock Exchange trading floor. Trading on the floor is by open outcry but is supplemented by a screen-based Automated Pit Trading System (APT) which extends the trading day by around 100 minutes. In addition, the Japanese Government Bond contract is traded on

14

APT throughout the day as it also provides a daytime trading environment for non-floor traded products, offering a cheaper way into a market for contracts that are likely to suffer from less liquidity at their outset.

The APT system was introduced in 1989 and uses a sophisticated and highly advanced technique to allow the open outcry pit trading mechanism to be represented electronically.

The contracts currently trading on LIFFE are as follows. (Contract specifications are given in Appendix A.)

> 3-month Ecu
> 1-month Euromark
> 3-month Euromark
> 3-month Eurodollar *(suspended in 1995)*
> 3-month Eurolire
> 3-month Euroswiss
> 3-month Sterling
> 3-month Euroyen
> Long Gilt
> German Government Bond (Bund)
> German Government Bond (Bobl)
> Italian Government Bond (BTP)
> Japanese Government Bond (JGB)
> FTSE 100 Stock Index
> FTSE 100 Flex Option
> FTSE Mid-250 Stock Index
> and Equity Options on 72 leading UK companies

In addition to the above contracts, a US financial contract was listed from May 1997 as part of an historic open outcry linkage between LIFFE and CBOT and their respective clearing houses. It was hoped to have started sooner but the technological problems encountered were enormous, particularly between the two clearing houses. Under the agreement, CBOT futures and options on the 30-year US Treasury Bond contract will trade on LIFFE's trading floor for 5½ hours before Chicago opens and LIFFE's German Government Bond (Bund) contract will trade on CBOT's trading floor for 3½ hours after London's close. The second phase of the linkage will feature the introduction on LIFFE of the US 10-year and 5-year Treasury Note contracts while CBOT will introduce LIFFE's UK and Italian Government Bond contracts.

The three-month Euroyen contract, launched in April 1996, is the culmination of an innovative link agreement with the Tokyo International Financial Futures Exchange (TIFFE) and is fully fungible with the TIFFE contract. This means that Euroyen contracts entered into on LIFFE will, at the end of the trading day, be transferred to TIFFE and will be replaced by equivalent TIFFE contracts. Other similar link-ups can be expected over the next few years.

In November 1996, as part of its preparations for European Monetary Union (EMU), LIFFE launched a one-month Euromark contract. The Exchange is determined to enhance its range of products in the run-up to EMU, particularly along the Deutschmark yield curve. All contracts affected by EMU will settle against Euro interest rates.

It is proposed to transfer trading in equity options onto the APT system as soon as the relevant technology is in place. This is the first time that a whole product line has been switched from open outcry onto an automated system and the reason for it is to increase transparency in the cash market. Hitherto, futures prices tended to lag behind the underlying cash securities they are derived from and the stock exchanges in trying to get trades published more quickly. LIFFE aims to establish a fully integrated order-driven automated market in which users can trade both cash and equity derivatives through a single screen. This means the setting-up of a new ATP-Plus trading system which is now being tested. Unforeseen problems have, however, delayed its implementation.

LIFFE merged with the London Commodity Exchange (LCE) in September 1996 and, since then, the two exchanges have been operating with a unified administration.

The LCE is Europe's leading centre for the trading of soft commodity derivatives. Established in its present form in 1954 on the resumption of futures trading after the Second World War, cocoa was the first soft commodity to trade (actually having started in 1952), followed by sugar in 1956 and coffee in 1958. These three commodities, with wool and rubber, formed the basis of the LCE at that time. The last two have since been de-listed through lack of interest. (Wool is actively traded on the Sydney Futures Exchange.) Over the years several other contracts were introduced, with varying degrees of success. These included cotton, fishmeal, soyabean oil and sunflowerseed oil.

Throughout the 1960s and 1970s, aided by frosts, diseases and other natural disasters, operations expanded rapidly and the markets twice had to move to bigger premises. At present, the trading floors are situated at Commodity Quay, St Katherine's Dock. In the meantime, the energy markets had opened and shared premises. The reorganisation and liberalisation of the City of London's financial institutions in 1986 saw the merging of the separate cocoa, coffee and sugar markets to form the London Commodity Exchange (1986) Limited, a Recognised Investment Exchange under the Financial Services Act of that year, moving into its current purpose-built location the following year.

In 1991, the LCE merged with the Baltic Futures Exchange, adding wheat, barley, potatoes and dry cargo freight futures (BIFFEX) contracts to the list.

The main method of trading on the LCE is by open outcry, although white and raw sugar futures are traded on the Exchange's automated trading system (FAST). FAST started in 1987 with the launching of the new white sugar contract, and raws were transferred in 1991. At that time, it was thought that automated trading would replace the open outcry method but opinion has swung back again and the latter method is enjoying a revival of support.

The two main advantages of screen-based trading over the open outcry method are the lower costs involved in setting up new contracts and its global reach, which enables it to embrace overseas markets. It also allows trading to take place round the clock as discussed in Chapter 2 and can lead to mutual offsetting and clearing. Its disadvantages include the demise of face-to-face confrontation where there is more scope for speculation and short-term manipulation to trigger a chart point or assumed stop loss orders, thereby generating added liquidity.

All contracts are cleared through the London Clearing House (LCH), which also acts as principal to both sides of every contract, thereby granting the maximum security to both parties.

Contracts currently traded on the LCE are cocoa, coffee, white and raw sugar (which is currently tradeless), potatoes, wheat, barley and dry cargo freight (BIFFEX). Specifications are listed in Appendix A. Amongst new contracts being considered for the future are olive oil, rapeseed and a revamped wheat futures contract.

The raw sugar contract has been a considerable thorn in the side of the Exchange for a number of years. In 1979, a new contract was launched, denominated in US currency; this continued until 1984 when it was superseded by an FOB contract (known as the No. 6 contract). In retrospect, the decision to change to a dollar-denominated contract appeared to herald the beginning of the demise of raw sugar trading in London. It effectively wiped out arbitrage trading which was a major source of income; volumes fell dramatically after 1989, from 155 875 lots in September of that year, to only 371 lots in January 1993. It ceased trading in April 1993.

Nevertheless, brokers and traders still demanded a raw sugar contract, so later the same year, the present – No. 7 – contract was launched. This has only minor modifications from the No. 6 contract and was placed, along with the white (No. 5) contract, on the Exchange's FAST system. This has not worked either and all futures business in raw sugar is now done on the New York market. Apart from the occasional spot trade, the No. 7 contract, which is known as the Premium Raw Sugar contract because it trades at a variable premium to the New York contract, is tradeless. The white sugar contract was launched in 1987 and is far more successful, enjoying soaring volumes in 1994/5.

Every morning, a benchmark spot price is set by a committee of traders and brokers. After consultation, and after taking into consideration all available bids and offers of physical parcels as well as any alterations to freight rates, etc, they fix what is known as the London Daily Price (LDP), one for raws and one for whites. Not only do these prices facilitate the pricing of physical contracts on maturity but they are also used extensively by governments and other bodies for other purposes, such as the fixing of subsidiaries by the European Community.

The LCE's coffee contract was changed to a dollar-denominated one in March 1991, but this did not affect turnover and it continues to trade very successfully.

Following an ill-fated attempt to launch a property futures market, the LCE was in a bad way in the early 1990s. In 1991, it needed a daily turnover of 21 000 lots to break even and was actually trading around half that number; two years later, this had been reduced to 9 600. However, in July 1993, LCE announced its first profit for three years. A significant increase in membership began to create a firm foundation and had seemed to lessen the likelihood of a takeover. Indeed, the Exchange was hoping to strengthen its ties with other exchanges both in London and overseas. These trends are discussed in Chapter 12. However, the LCE was taken over by LIFFE in September 1996.

The International Petroleum Exchange (IPE)

The IPE was incorporated in November 1980 and its first contract, gasoil futures, was launched early in 1981. This contract called for physical delivery by warrant but, in response to demands from the trade, it was changed to an FOB basis in 1984. Around that time, there were also attempts to launch gasoline, heavy fuel oil and Brent crude oil contracts but they failed to generate sufficient support and had to be abandoned. However, in June 1988, a new cash-settled Brent Crude Oil contract was relaunched and this enjoys considerable success. It is based on the 15-day Brent Crude forward market, one of the most widely traded forward crude oil markets in the world. Recent physical developments have considerably expanded its base, further improving future prospects.

The concept of cash settlement in energy futures has now been accepted within the industry as a flexible and efficient method of settlement, as it eliminates the problems and paperwork associated with physical delivery. This method does not exclude those who require to make or take delivery of physical oil; this is done by the Exchange for Physicals (EFP) system. EFPs are also an effective means of price risk management; they can be hedged against a future position as a protection against future adverse price movements. The EFP system has also actually increased volume on the IPE as it encourages pricing contracts and can also be used as a differential pricing mechanism to separate pricing and physical supply arrangements.

Options have also been successfully introduced on both the gasoil and Brent crude futures contracts. These cover the first six months traded on the underlying futures contracts. In 1992, the IPE introduced its own options price-reporting system which has considerably increased turnover in options trading.

Other contracts were launched in the early 1990s but these have yet to make an impact. The Dubai Sour Crude contract was launched in July 1990 but has yet to gain liquidity; the IPE is committed to the development of a sour crude contract, so this should eventually succeed.

An unleaded gasoline contract was launched in January 1992. This is well supported by the trade and competes with the successful NYMEX contract.

In February 1997, a natural gas contract was launched. Developed in consultation with industry, it is designed around individual daily deliveries, although they may be traded in groups such as calendar months. Trading is done electronically via the IPE's Energy Trading System (ETS), with the LCH becoming the counterparty to all trades. The IPE is also looking at the possibilities of electricity and coal futures trading but that does not seem likely to happen in the immediate future.

All contracts are cleared through the LCH, incorporating the Standard Portfolio Analysis of Risk (SPAN) margining system. Contract specifications are given in Appendix A.

The London Metal Exchange (LME)

The LME was originally established in 1877, acquiring its own premises in Whittington Avenue in 1882. In those days, the only metals traded were copper, tin and pig-iron. Trading was initially conducted around a chalk line drawn on the floor. That line was the origin of The Ring, the present-day five-minute official trading periods.

Even in those days, things developed fast: strict times for trading were quickly established and official contracts approved. Three months was standardised in 1883 as the forward trading date, as that was the approximate sailing time from Santiago and Singapore to the UK, for copper and tin respectively. Daily prompt dates were needed to allow for the adjusting of contract dates to overcome the vagaries of ships' arrivals.

Except for periods of closure during the two World Wars, trading on the LME flourished. In 1980, after 98 years in Whittington Avenue, it moved to Plantation House and then, 14 years later, to its present home at 56 Leadenhall Street. Copper and tin have traded at the LME since 1882: the copper contract was upgraded to High Grade in 1981 and to Grade A in 1986; the tin contract, after a short closure following the collapse of the International Tin Council (see Chapter 8), was upgraded to 99.85% purity and restarted in 1989. Lead and zinc were officially introduced in 1920. The lead contract, apart from a change to US dollar denominations, has remained virtually intact, but zinc has undergone several changes, following alterations to trading patterns and end-users' wishes. The present contract is Special High Grade (SHG) 99.995% pure, which has been trading since 1986. Primary aluminium started off as a 99.5% contract but was upgraded to 99.7% High Grade in 1987. Nickel commenced trading in 1979 and aluminium alloy in 1992. Full contract specifications are given in Appendix A.

The present arrangement of dealing in two periods, or 'Rings' as they are called, each morning and afternoon was introduced in 1899. The LME is not a futures market in the traditional sense – it is more a forward market, as it has specific delivery dates as opposed to periods of up to a month such as futures enjoy. As a forward market, metals are traded daily for the first three months. For periods over three months there are weekly or monthly prompt dates, depending on how long into the future the contract extends. Contracts can be traded up to 27 months ahead but it is not until the final three months that they are traded daily.

Trading takes place during the Ring, on the 'kerb' or inter-office, depending on the time of day. Any transactions done outside Ring dealing times must be reported to the LME immediately. Ring dealing times, each of which last for exactly five minutes, are as follows:

Morning Session	*Afternoon Session*
11.45 aluminium alloy	15.20 lead
11.50 tin	15.25 zinc
11.55 primary aluminium	15.30 copper
12.00 copper	15.35 primary aluminium
12.05 lead	15.40 tin
12.10 zinc	15.45 nickel
12.15 nickel	15.50 aluminium alloy
12.30 copper	16.00 lead
12.40 tin	16.05 zinc
12.45 lead	16.10 copper

12.50 zinc	16.15 primary aluminium
12.55 primary aluminium	16.20 tin
13.00 nickel	16.25 nickel
13.05 aluminium alloy	16.30 aluminium alloy

Kerb trading takes place from 13.10 to 13.30 and from 16.35 to 17.00. At all other times, trading is conducted from members' offices.

Daily, at 13.30, after the morning kerb, the official prices are declared; these are based on the prices prevailing at the end of the second Ring of the morning. These official prices are important as they form the basis of many physical contracts. The bulk of the international metals trade is handled through physical contracts negotiated direct by producers and consumers, but these contracts involve only the quality and quantity of metal to be supplied in the future – the actual prices are based on other official prices; this can, therefore, lead to a certain amount of manoeuvring and manipulating at some second morning Rings.

Settlement of LME contracts is by warrant, with the metal concerned lying in an approved warehouse and of an approved brand listed by the LME. The LME posts the tonnage of the metals that are held in LME-approved warehouses every day. This gives a good indication of the fundamental position of a market and can influence the price. However, the system is not foolproof as any member can move a substantial tonnage into or out of an approved warehouse on a temporary basis, in order to influence the price in the short term. Following the Financial Services Act (FSA) 1986, the LME switched from a principal's market to a centrally cleared one. This was forced upon them by the FSA and also in the aftermath of the tin crisis of 1985, when confidence was severely dented. This meant that contracts were henceforth guaranteed by the LCH instead of by the buyers and sellers themselves.

The fact that the LME is not a futures market in the truest sense of the word does not preclude it from attracting the speculator; opportunities for huge profits and losses are just as readily available here as on other futures markets. Although there have been many complaints about the adverse influence of speculators on the LME, they are just as valuable here as in other markets.

The LME has a system of large position reporting in order to deal with any excessive manipulation or price squeezes in an orderly way. The committee has the power to impose limits on the levels at which metal can be borrowed or lent for a day if it discovers any untoward activities. This calms the market but does, of course, have the effect of limiting the losses of those caught in the squeeze which, some say, defeats the object of a completely free market. A truly free market should be able to handle squeezes without restraint.

There have been several instances during the 1990s when it has been necessary to impose such limits, most notably on the copper and zinc markets. At the time of the Sumitomo scandal in 1996, when its chief copper trader was found to have manipulated the market to such an extent that the price rose over $1000 per tonne more than it should have done, the LME committee imposed a daily trading limit that remained in force for many months and may prove to be semi-permanent.

Average price options for copper and aluminium were introduced in February 1997. It was hoped to start them back in 1993 but, as they are non-deliverable, they did not conform to the LME ethos and might have contravened EU legislation. However, it appears that if, as they mature, they are converted to a straight futures or options contract, they would be deemed to be deliverable, so the problems appear now to have been surmounted. Traded Average Price Options (TAPOS), as they are known, are already offered to investors by LME members as Over the Counter (OTC) instruments but exchange-traded TAPOS would have greater liquidity, transparency and efficiency as well as the protection of the LCH and regulatory bodies. Copper and primary aluminium will be the first two contracts to be launched with the others following if they prove successful. These contracts, which are European style options in that they cannot be declared early, will be based on the LME monthly average settlement price (MASP).

They are designed to complement the present futures and options contracts; users of the market who use MASPs to trade will find these very useful. However, hedgers who currently use the flexible daily prompt system will continue to use the old system. It is hoped that TAPOS will recover some business lost to the OTC market.

Plans for the future include the eventual introduction of a stainless steel contract. Work has been going on for a long time to finalise this but there are still many obstacles to be overcome, so its launch may not be imminent.

The London Bullion Market Association (LBMA)

Although the gold market is a truly global one, London is still the leader, with its long-established fixing system. In the majority of dealings, gold is also cleared on a *loco* London basis.

The LBMA is a trade association, not a futures exchange, but it plays an important role in the trading of gold, so a rudimentary knowledge of its workings is essential. Following the Financial Services Act of 1986, when the Bank of England took over supervisory responsibility for the bullion market, the LBMA was formed.

Prior to that, and since 1919, there were only five members who formed a fixing committee, meeting twice a day in Rothschild's offices to fix the a.m. and p.m. gold bullion prices. This task is still done by five members who differ little from the original five. These are: NM Rothschild, Samuel Montagu, Mocatta and Goldsmid, Sharps Pixley and Mase Westpac.

At 10.30 a.m. and 3.00 p.m. every working day, this committee, in constant contact with their dealing rooms – which in turn are in touch with traders and clients around the world – meets to determine the 'London Fix', an internationally recognised yardstick at which millions of dollars of physical gold contracts are settled each day. The fix begins with the Chairman naming a price on the basis of pre-fix trading activity. That is relayed back to the dealing rooms, which respond with bids and offers from customers. Prices are settled and if there is a surplus of buyers, the price is raised (lowered if a surplus of sellers). This continues until all bids and offers are catered for; all the deals are done at the last price, which is the official fixing price. Usually the process takes only minutes but has been known to take over two hours when the market is particularly active.

Up until the beginning of 1997, the workings of the LBMA were veiled in a wave of secrecy and the size of the market was unknown. However, in January of 1997, the LBMA lifted the veil to reveal that the size of its market was very big indeed. Around 30 million ounces of gold, worth about $10 billion is cleared every working day and this does not include any in-house netting of orders by the five members, so the true figure is much bigger.

The London Securities and Derivatives Exchange (OMLX)

Inaugurated in December 1989, OMLX is the only fully computerised derivatives exchange in London. Initially, the Exchange was created to trade Swedish financial products but expanded, by popular demand, to attract a large London following. In 1993, the name OMLX was first introduced to the London market.

OMLX trades Swedish equity indices and is linked to OM Stockholm; it is also part of the FEX (First European Exchanges) Alliance. Its link with OM Stockholm was the first instance in the world of two exchanges electronically connected. The success of this link became the blueprint for further such linkages and led to the creation of the FEX Alliance, set up in 1992. Other members of the FEX Alliance are OM Stockholm, EOE-Optiebeurs Amsterdam, Swiss Options and Financial Futures Exchange (SOFFEX) and the Austrian Futures and Options Exchanges (OTOB).

Contracts traded on OMLX are the OMX Index, the Long OMX Index and Swedish stocks. Specifications are given in Appendix A. The Exchange is also considering electricity futures and plans to launch a pulp futures market in 1997. Unlike the pulp contract launched in Helsinki in early 1997, it will be based on physical delivery, but using the same basis for the contract – northern bleached softwood kraft (NBSK), an industry benchmark.

The Chicago Board of Trade (CBOT)

The CBOT was formed in 1848 principally to trade forward contracts, allowing buyers and sellers of agricultural commodities to specify delivery of a particular commodity at a predetermined price and date. These contracts, however, had their drawbacks as they were not fully standardised and certain merchants took advantage of this deficiency by failing to deliver or otherwise defaulting on their obligations.

In order to combat this, the CBOT took steps to formalise grain trading by developing contracts standardised with respect to quality, quantity and delivery. These were the first futures contracts, where the only variable was the price. Standardisation of contract terms led to the rapidly increased use of the futures markets by the grain trade and also attracted speculators who saw the opportunities offered by taking the other side, either short or long. Speculators made the markets more liquid and minimised price fluctuations by shortening the bid and offer spreads made by the traders.

Although early records were lost in the Great Chicago Fire of 1871, it is accepted that, by 1865, most of the basic principles of futures trading – as we know them today – were in place, including margining and clearing.

The first contracts traded on the CBOT were corn (maize), wheat and oats. Soyabeans followed in 1936, soyabean oil in 1950 and soyabean meal in 1951. In the early 1970s, currencies were allowed to float. This, along with the explosion of US government-issued debt, moved the world economy away from a relatively stable interest-rate scenario to one that was much more volatile. The CBOT's first financial futures contracts were Government National Mortgage Association Certificates (GNMAs), which began trading in 1975. US Treasury Bonds were launched two years later and are now by far the most active of the Exchange's contracts; indeed, it is the second most active contract in the world after the Chicago Mercantile Exchange's (CME) Eurodollar contract.

Other financial contracts followed, including municipal bond index futures and fixed-term Treasury notes. The 1990s saw the launch of fertiliser futures, and catastrophe and crop yield insurance futures. Yield

Curve Spread Futures, a contract based on the differences between yields in long and short term treasury securities, were launched in October 1996. Ten different contracts are offered with varying yield relationships which enable investors to take a view on inflation and other economic developments. These latter are rather specialised contracts and they still suffer from very low volumes. Full specifications of all the CBOT's contracts are given in Appendix A.

The CBOT's first options contract was a Treasury Bond futures and began trading in 1982. This soon led to the opening of options on other financial contracts as well as the agricultural ones. There are now options on virtually all the futures contracts. Following the CME's lead, the CBOT launched an emerging market bond index contract in 1996.

The Mid America Commodity Exchange (MIDAM)

MIDAM is an affiliate of the CBOT. Under this affiliation, which was approved by the Commodities and Futures Trading Commission (CFTC) in 1986, MIDAM remains a separate legal entity and a separate exchange. The CBOT is its sole voting member and provides the administration and support services for it.

Contracts on MIDAM mirror those of other exchanges in all but one respect: sizes are a half to a fifth in comparison. Those traded are the same as on the CME and COMEX (Commodity Exchange) as well as CBOT. A full list, with specifications, appears in Appendix A. The MIDAM exchange exists for the very small trader but is not well supported. Average daily volumes in 1995 reached four figures in only three contracts: corn (maize), soyabeans and Treasury bonds.

The Chicago Mercantile Exchange (CME)

The CME was founded as the Chicago Produce Exchange in 1874. To improve its image and better to reflect its presence, it changed its name to the Chicago Mercantile Exchange in 1919. At this time, fledgling European exchanges were beginning to reopen after the First World War and public awareness of and participation in futures exchanges were increasing. At the same time, a CME clearing house was established.

Until the Second World War, the CME traded futures on eggs, butter, cheese, potatoes and onions. Then, in 1945, it listed turkey futures, followed in later years by apples, poultry, frozen eggs, iron and steel scrap, but none of these contracts has survived to the present day. The oldest contract currently traded is frozen pork bellies, which began trading in 1961. This was followed in 1964 by a live cattle futures contract, live hogs in 1966 and feeder cattle in 1971. Lumber futures contracts were first introduced in 1969. The live hogs contract was replaced by a lean hogs contract in February 1997. A grade A milk futures contract was introduced in January 1996.

The demise of the Bretton Woods Agreement in 1971 heralded the advent of financial futures, the dawn of a new financial era. In May 1972, the CME inaugurated the International Monetary Market (IMM), a division created for financial futures trading. Contracts based on seven foreign currencies were launched. Ten years later, another division The Index and Options Market (IOM) of the CME was created to trade indices and options.

With the launch of the IOM's first contract, based on Standard and Poor's 500 Stock Index, futures trading became accessible to equity market participants, making the CME the most financially diversified exchange in the world. This diversification was carried further in 1995 with the creation of an emerging markets division, Growth and Emerging Markets (GEM), on which was launched a Mexican peso futures contract, followed by other emerging market currencies, interest rates and stock index futures. The end of 1996 saw the launch of Oriented Strand Board (OSB) futures and options. Dubbed the construction material of the future, it is an engineered wood product that competes with plywood in flooring, roofing and sheathing. A full list of contracts with their specifications is given in Appendix A.

In 1984, the CME became the first futures exchange to establish an international trading link; this mutual offset (MOS) arrangement with SIMEX was the first step towards the 24-hour market. The system, which runs until 1999, allows a member or customer of either exchange to transfer a position on one exchange to the clearing house of the other. The most popular contract for this activity is the CME's Eurodollar. In March 1996, Euroyen futures were launched under the market's MOS agreement. For the first time, therefore, the world's most popular non-US interest rate future began trading in both the US and Asian time zones. The two exchanges, CME and SIMEX, remain independently owned and operated, however, maintaining separate clearing houses and audits, compliance and surveillance departments. Future plans include the launch of a ground beef contract later in 1997.

The Chicago Board Options Exchange (CBOE)

The CBOE lists options on all the equity index contracts of other exchanges as well as over 700 stocks. It also offers interest rate options, LEAPS and FLEX options.

The New York Mercantile Exchange (NYMEX)

NYMEX was founded in 1872. Originally known as the Butter and Cheese Exchange, the establishment of a commercial exchange was essential to organise the distribution of agricultural produce efficiently and economically, and to protect the interests of dairy merchants. In an attempt to expand its scope, it changed its name in 1875 to the American Exchange of New York and succeeded in securing the egg trade. Rapid growth followed, attracting a large number of new members from other trades. As a result, it changed its name yet again in 1882, to that which it still holds today.

Futures trading gradually evolved during the first three decades of the 20th century and a clearing house was opened in 1924. Trading in dressed poultry was a feature of the 1930s and in potatoes during the 1940s, the latter largely forced upon the Exchange by wartime trading restrictions. Trading in butter and eggs steadily declined. New technology allowed chickens to lay eggs all the year round, causing hedging operations to lose their appeal. It was not until after the Second World War that potato trading really took off. Potatoes became NYMEX's most important commodity and remained so until 1976.

During this time, many new contracts – including apples, aluminium, rice and plywood – were launched, but most failed and were closed after a few years. Among the successes was platinum, which opened for trading in 1956 and was quickly accepted. By the 1960s, platinum had joined the potato contract as one of the mainstays of NYMEX. Trading grew rapidly when free trading in gold was established. Palladium trading began in 1968.

The 1970s saw the end of potato trading. For some years, the importance of the Maine potato crop had been waning. Production was declining and its role in determining the supply and demand balance diminished. The result was a contracting supply of deliverable stock to the market and a major default in 1976. Fifty million pounds of potatoes against 997 contracts expiring in May failed to be delivered. The effect on NYMEX was devastating and very nearly led to its enforced closure. Another crisis in 1979 was the final nail in the potato's coffin, and trading finally ceased in that year.

However, futures were spectacularly revived by the opening of the energy futures markets, and NYMEX was able to establish itself as the primary energy exchange in the 1980s. Heating oil began trading in 1978, crude oil in 1983, unleaded gasoline in 1984 and natural gas in 1990. Trading in these contracts expanded rapidly and NYMEX is now arguably the most important New York futures market.

Helping it to get to this position, it merged with COMEX in 1994. COMEX is the leading US metals futures market and has now become a division of NYMEX. Founded in 1933, it originally traded silver and copper futures. The current silver contract is the same as it was in 1933, but copper was relaunched in its present form in 1988. In 1983, an unsuccessful and short-lived aluminium contract was launched, and the Exchange's third successful contract, for gold, was launched in 1974. This, with silver and copper, comprises three very popular contracts. Following the merger, there are plans to relaunch an aluminium contract at some stage.

In March 1996, NYMEX launched the world's first electricity futures contracts. Two contracts were launched, identical in all respects except that one is based on delivery at the California–Oregon Border (COB) and the other at Palo Verde, Arizona (PV). An eastern US delivery point was added in Spring 1997 and others can be added at any time. The contracts are traded on the Exchange's Access after-hours computer trading system. Options started in April 1996, but are not traded on Access at time of writing. Many OTC trades are already being priced off the Dow-Jones-Cob index but this system will allow greater transparency, providing a way of managing the risks of fluctuating electricity prices caused by the deregulation of the US electricity industry.

Five-day options on the three successful metals contracts were introduced in the early 1990s but volumes are very low. In 1992, COMEX introduced a stock index contract, the Eurotop 100, comprising 100 of the most blue-chip stocks in nine European contracts.

COMEX copper futures were listed on NYMEX's Access electronic system in early 1995, substantially overlapping with the LME's trading hours. Competition between the two exchanges is intense but, when the LME opened approved warehouses in the USA in June 1995, volumes on COMEX suffered. Future plans include a possible coal futures contract in the second half of 1997.

The Coffee, Sugar and Cocoa Exchange (CSCE)

The CSCE commenced operations in 1881 as the Coffee Exchange of New York. It was founded by a group of coffee merchants anxious to rebuild their trade after uncontrolled speculation and a huge oversupply had caused its collapse two years earlier. It traded successfully – if unspectacularly – until 1916 when a sugar contract was launched.

The established sugar exchanges of London and Hamburg closed down during the First World War and the New York exchange was quick to fill the gap, changing its name, naturally enough, to the New York Coffee and Sugar Exchange. In 1925, the New York Cocoa Exchange was founded, establishing a market for cocoa in parallel to coffee. It was the world's first exchange for cocoa.

In 1979, the two exchanges merged to form the present body. In 1982, the CSCE became the first US exchange to trade options when they were introduced on the Sugar No. 11 contract. Options on the coffee and cocoa contracts followed in 1986.

In 1985 a domestic sugar contract (known as the No. 14 contract) was launched and, in 1987, a white sugar was also launched. Both these contracts have a very limited volume nowadays but the No. 11 world sugar contract has proved to be truly a worldwide contract, as volumes have dried up in London. In June 1996, the Exchange launched a new world wide white sugar contract, deliverable FOB from ports in 33 countries.

The present cocoa contract has not changed since 1925, but the current coffee 'C' contract was launched only in 1964. In 1992 a new coffee contract was launched, designed to run in parallel, in the form of a freight differential one, based on Brazilian coffee. This has not proved to be a success and is currently tradeless.

In 1993, the CSCE introduced two new contracts based on dairy products; these cheddar cheese and non-fat dried milk contracts are taking time to becoming accepted and volumes in early 1996 were very low. Grade A milk futures were launched in December 1995. Non-storable and regionally marketed, it is a surprising choice for a futures market, but the Exchange is determined to build up a dairy division with its own range of dairy contracts. A butter contract was added in October 1996. Contract specifications are given in Appendix A.

The New York Cotton Exchange (NYCE)

Founded in 1870, the NYCE is New York's oldest commodity exchange. Trading only cotton until 1966, it reflected the importance of the cotton trade in the 19th and early 20th centuries. In 1966, it founded the Citrus Associates to launch a frozen concentrated orange juice contract, and in 1985 entered the world of financial futures with the creation of FINEX.

The New York Futures Exchange (NYFE), a wholly-owned subsidiary of the New York Stock Exchange, merged with the NYCE in 1993, adding two valuable index contracts to its list. The NYFE is an automated trading exchange and opened in 1985.

Specifications for all these contracts are given in Appendix A.

The Philadelphia Stock Exchange (PHLX)

North America's oldest securities market formed a financial futures affiliate in 1982, launching options contracts on Deutschmarks, Swiss francs, Canadian dollars and Japanese yen. Futures contracts were added later.

Primarily an options exchange, PHLX now covers many more currencies and introduced cross-rate options from 1991. These contracts are designed as a new additional and versatile financial vehicle for hedging or speculation. In November 1994, PHLX introduced the United Currency Options Market (UCOM) to give more flexibility to the options. Virtual currency (dollar-denominated delivery) options were introduced at the same time. These call for settlement in US dollars, giving US investors the opportunity to settle up in their own currency, thereby avoiding expensive bank lines to trade the underlying currency. Contract specifications are given in Appendix A.

The Kansas City Board of Trade (KCBOT)

Founded in 1856, futures trading on the KCBOT began with wheat in 1876. The present hard red winter wheat contract was launched 100 years later and options were introduced in 1984. Meanwhile, in 1982, after several years of negotiation with the CFTC, trading started in the Value Line index, a securities index covering nearly 1700 stocks. The following year, a smaller version was launched, known as the Mini Value Line.

In 1995, KCBOT launched a natural gas contract. Designed to reflect activity west of the Mississippi, it is a Western Natural Gas contract. All contract specifications are given in Appendix A.

The Minneapolis Grain Exchange (MGE)

Originally called the Minneapolis Chamber of Commerce, the MGE was founded in 1881 and has been a central market-place for grain produced in the surrounding areas ever since. It boasts the largest cash grain market in the world. The hard red spring wheat contract was launched in 1893 and the white wheat in 1984. White and black tiger shrimp contracts were launched in 1993 and 1994, respectively but were slow to catch on and volumes were low at the outset. Contract specifications can be found in Appendix A.

Marché à Terme International de France (MATIF)

MATIF was founded in 1986 and quickly became a remarkable success. Originally a financial futures market, in 1988 it took over the sugar, coffee and cocoa contracts traded in Paris. Since then, the cocoa and coffee contracts have been de-listed due to lack of interest, but the white sugar one remains successful.

MATIF's first financial contract was the Notional Long-Term Bond, launched in 1986, representing several seven- to ten-year government bonds. It was an instant success and was followed by the 3-month PIBOR (Paris interbank) and CAC40, a stock index futures contract, two years later. MATIF is now the fourth-largest futures and options exchange in the world. Contract specifications are given in Appendix A.

MATIF is, at time of writing, the only European exchange that is a member of Globex, the 24-hour trading system set up by CME and Reuters, and it contributes strongly to its turnover. It plans to leave it, however, when its current contract expires in 1998. As part of the increasing internationalisation of futures markets, MATIF signed a co-operation agreement with Germany's Deutsche Terminbörse (DTB) in 1993 to link the two markets electronically. Full implementation of the link-up was, however, delayed by technical problems and had to be abandoned in 1996. There was also the thorny problem of giving up MATIF's traditional open outcry trading method – something the members were very reluctant to do.

MATIF also trades potato and rapeseed futures – the latter having been launched in 1995 – while wheat futures trading started in July 1996, made possible by the lifting of a ban on wheat speculation dating back to 1936. The slow but steady reform of the EU's Common Agricultural Policy should open up new avenues for increased trade.

Future plans include a 100 ICUMSA white sugar contract in 1997 and Euro-denominated financial contracts in 1998. In its efforts to secure a sizeable share of the market in the run-up to EMU and beyond, MATIF will ensure it has the right contracts. Some existing contracts may have to be converted.

There is also a separate options market in France, the Marché des Options Négociables de Paris, or MONEP, where options on the CAC40 are traded, together with equity options on around 50 of the country's leading stocks. In 1996, it gained approval from the US Securities Exchange Commission (SEC) to market its CAC40 options contract in the USA.

Deutsche Terminbörse (DTB)

Established in 1989, trading started on the DTB in January 1990 with options on the stocks of 14 leading companies. It is an electronic trading market, with members being part of a nation-wide network of trading terminals.

By the end of 1990, two futures contracts had been launched: the long-term government bond (bund) and the German stock index (DAX) contracts. These were followed by the medium-term government bond – or BOBL – contract the following year. Options were soon added.

In 1994, a FIBOR (Frankfurt Interbank Offered Rate) contract was launched and this is enjoying moderate success. Less successful was the 30-year government bond contract launched the same year; known as the BUXL, it had to be scrapped after just over a year. At the end of 1996, the DTB introduced a one-month Euromark contract as part of its preparations for EMU. A three-month Euromark was launched in early 1997 and a two-year one is planned. Contract specifications are given in Appendix A.

DTB had plans to launch a DM/$ currency option in 1996, denominated in dollars (unlike similar products on CME or PHLX, which are denominated in Deutschmarks). Permission has been gained from the CFTC to place its trading screens in the USA. The DTB follows a policy of taking its products to the customer, rather than expansion through offering a wider range of products, taking advantage of the liberalisation of trade between European countries brought about by the EU's Investors Services Directive (ISD). As a result, the exchange has opened access points in several countries, including the UK.

Germany's first commodity futures market is due to open in Hanover in 1997. Called the Deutsche Warenterminbörse, it plans to start off with wheat and hog contracts (and possibly a scrap paper futures contract, which would be the world's first).

Other European exchanges

It has become something of a status symbol in Europe to have a futures and options market and nearly every country has one. Most offer a government bond contract, an equity index one and/or an interest rate one. Not all are open to overseas investors. The following countries currently have derivative markets: Austria, Belgium, Denmark, Finland, Holland, Hungary, Ireland, Italy, Norway, Poland, Portugal, Spain, Sweden and Switzerland. Specifications of the most active contracts are given in Appendix A and the addresses of the exchanges in Appendix B. Greece and Turkey are also considering opening futures exchanges.

In mid-1996, MEFFRF (Meff Renta Fijal–Spain) launched a new type of board derivative – a price differential futures contract, or DIFF, which allows traders to trade the price differentials between the Spanish 10-year bond future and its French, Italian and German equivalents. Finland, despite the failure of similar ventures in Canada and Sweden, launched a pulp futures contract in early 1997. This should be followed by OMLX in London with a similar contract and the possibility of one in Hanover in 1997/8.

In February 1997, the Norwegian and Swedish Exchanges, together with OMLX in London, began a joint trading and clearing operation. This is symptomatic of the need to cut costs and remain competitive in the run-up to EMU. Other such link-ups can be expected in the future.

The EU directives that came into force in January 1996 enable banks and brokers to trade in any member-state's market without a physical presence in that country provided they are properly regulated in their own country. This is likely slowly to revolutionise these exchanges and some of the smaller ones may be unable to survive. London, Paris and Frankfurt seem likely to get the bulk of the business, provided, of course, that they have suitably popular contracts.

The Winnipeg Commodity Exchange (WCE)

The WCE is Canada's oldest and largest futures exchange. Its flaxseed and oats contracts first traded in 1904 and have remained unchanged ever since. Rye was added in 1917 but de-listed in 1995. There are now seven agricultural contracts: flaxseed, oats, canola and peas are traded for domestic and international use, and wheat, barley and western barley are traded for domestic use only. Contract specifications are given in Appendix A.

The canola (Canadian oil low acid) contract superseded a rapeseed contract in 1988. It is a derivative of rapeseed and has the lowest saturated fat content of all edible fats and oils. The Exchange is contemplating a hog futures contract for 1997/8.

Other Canadian exchanges

There are four other Canadian exchanges: the Montreal Exchange (ME), Toronto Futures Exchange (TFE) and the Toronto and Vancouver Stock Exchanges (TSE and VSE). The last three trade mainly equity instruments but the VSE also trades gold options. The TFE was set up in 1980 as a division of the TSE and became a separate entity four years later.

Founded in 1982, the ME trades three government bond contracts and two Canadian bankers acceptance futures as well as a couple of equity option instruments. Contract specifications can be found in Appendix A.

ME's most successful contract is the three-month bankers acceptance interest rate future, known as the BAX. Apart from that contract, financial instrument volumes do not compare favourably with comparable centres such as Sydney, Australia.

Bolsa de Mercadorias & Futuros (BM&F)

There are several fledgling derivatives markets in Central and South America – notably in Mexico, Argentina and Chile – but Brazil's BM&F is by far the biggest. Of its four financial contracts, two of them are among the top five in the world in terms of volume. Its US dollar contract was third in 1995, with an average daily turnover of over 303 000 lots, and its one-day interbank deposits contract is fifth, with over 143 000 lots per day.

Founded in 1985, it started operations the following year with a gold and a stock option (IBOVESPA) contract. The hugely successful US dollar contract was launched in 1987 and the one-day interbank in 1991. BM&F currently has a total of 15 contracts of varying size and liquidity and is the third largest futures exchange in the world. Full details of the contracts are given in Appendix A, including coffee, cattle and cotton. In 1995, three more were launched: a reconstituted soyabean contract, crystal sugar and flexible currency. Soyabeans were first introduced in 1993 but support was lacking; it was consequently relaunched in October 1995, as a slightly smaller contract (27 tonnes instead of 30) with fewer delivery months (five instead of eight).

There are plans for a maize contract to be launched in 1997 and there is talk of an alcohol contract. The exchange also aims to launch a contract in Brazilian debt, although reliable value quotations could prove difficult to obtain. By far the most active emerging market derivatives exchange, BM&F is in a unique position. However, emerging market business is coveted by foreign competition; the two biggest Chicago exchanges have already listed Brady bonds. The CME launched a Brazilian C (capitalisation) bond in March 1996. Three days later BM&F launched its own C-bond and immediately grabbed 96% of the total C-bond trading by value. Contract sizes tend to be smaller on BM&F and this attracts much extra business. Perhaps there is a lesson to be learned here.

The Sydney Futures Exchange (SFE)

The SFE was founded in 1960. Originally known as the Sydney Greasy Wool Futures Exchange, it dropped 'Greasy Wool' from its title in 1972. Until 1975, it traded only wool; however, in that year a cattle contract was launched. This was followed, in 1978, by a gold contract – the first to be launched outside North America. Cattle and gold contracts are no longer listed, while the wool contract was relaunched in 1995. Wheat futures started trading in 1996. The SFE's first financial contract was listed in 1979; 90-day Bank Bills was the first financial futures contract outside the USA. In 1983, a stock index contract was launched, and trading links with LIFFE and COMEX were established in 1986, followed by NYMEX and CBOT in 1995.

In 1989, SFE launched an overnight screen dealing system known as SYCOM, and in 1991 the Exchange's own clearing house commenced operations. In 1994, SFE launched share futures on seven leading individual shares, with three more the following year. To date, the SFE is the only exchange to offer futures on individual shares. Contract specifications are given in Appendix A.

Plans are afoot to increase the commodity side of operations with a revival of the gold contract and the introduction of silver and copper futures. It is hoped to launch these, through its new electronic link with NYMEX, which is also used for crude oil trading. The contracts will be traded simultaneously on NYMEX's Access and SFE's SYCOM. The authorities are also studying the feasibility of launching a coal futures contract.

The New Zealand Futures and Options Exchange (NZFOE)

The NZFOE was established in 1985 and became a subsidiary of the SFE on 31 December 1992. It provides only a screen dealing system and has no trading floor. It trades five financial and equity index contracts as well as a wool contract. Specifications are given in Appendix A.

It has plans to launch electricity futures trading.

Japanese futures exchanges

Until 1996, there were 11 futures exchanges in Japan; the business was very fragmented but the liberalisation and deregulation of the country's financial markets that year enabled the mergers of some of the smaller exchanges to go ahead. It also enabled foreigners to participate in the Japanese futures markets. The three Nagoya exchanges merged in October 1996 and the Kansai Grain and Silk ones in April 1997. Other mergers, later in 1997, are likely to be Kobe Rubber/Osaka textiles and Yokohama silk/Maebashi silk.

Futures trading in Japan can be traced back to 1730 when rice futures were traded at the Dojima rice market. From 1870, they were traded on the forerunner of the Tokyo Grain Exchange, undergoing extensive modernisation in 1893 to include cotton, sugar and raw silk trading. During the Second World War, trading on all commodity exchanges was suspended; a new law reviving the trade was passed in 1950. Two years later, the industry was again thriving.

The most active markets are the Tokyo International Financial Futures Exchange (TIFFE), the Tokyo Grain Exchange (TGE), the Tokyo Commodity Exchange (TOCOM) and the Osaka Securities Exchange (OSE).

TIFFE was founded in 1989 with the launch of three-month Euroyen and Eurodollar contracts; the former is very successful, averaging over 150 000 contracts a day, while the latter was tradeless at the end of 1995. In 1990, a US$/yen contract started trading, followed by a one-year Euroyen one in 1992. Details of these and all other leading Japanese contracts can be found in Appendix A.

Trading on TGE began in 1952. In 1993 it merged with the Tokyo Sugar Exchange and two years later it absorbed the Hokkaido Grain Exchange. Currently, US soyabeans, corn (maize), red beans and raw sugar futures are traded.

TOCOM was established in 1984 from a merger of the Tokyo textile, rubber and gold exchanges, founded in 1951, 1952 and 1982, respectively. Cotton yarn started trading in 1951 and rubber in 1952. Following the launch of gold in 1982, other precious metals quickly followed. Gold, platinum and rubber are still very active markets. Other successful contracts are silver and palladium, while aluminium was launched in April 1997 and gasoline is planned for 1998.

The OSE started trading in 1988 with a Nikkei 225 Stock Index futures contract, with options following a year later. This was followed in 1994 by a Nikkei 300 contract. The former was made famous as one leg of an arbitrage operation traded by Baring's 'rogue trader' Nick Leeson. The other leg was a similar contract in Singapore.

Other financial and index contracts are traded on the Tokyo Stock Exchange (TSE), which runs a very successful ten-year Japanese Government Bond contract, to which was added, in 1996, a five-year one. A stock price index is also traded. Commodity contracts are also traded on the Kansai Agricultural Commodities Exchange (KANEX) – sugar and beans – and the Kobe Rubber Exchange (KRE).

The Singapore International Monetary Exchange (SIMEX)

SIMEX was founded in 1984 as a mainly financial futures market, launching Eurodollar, gold, Deutschmark and – after two months – yen contracts. Since then it has expanded into other spheres, offering a diverse range of contracts showing an innovativeness lacking in most other Pacific-area markets.

SIMEX has its origins in the Gold Exchange of Singapore (GES) and was Asia's first financial futures exchange. It also scored two other notable firsts, becoming Asia's first energy futures market with the launch in 1989 of its high-sulphur fuel oil contract, while in 1986 it made history when it launched the world's first futures contract based on the Japanese stock market, the Nikkei 225 Index future.

On its inauguration, SIMEX pioneered what is only now, in the mid-1990s, becoming more common – a mutual offset system (MOS). This international trading link with the CME offers extended trading hours across different time zones, increased risk management opportunities and, above all, reduced transaction costs. In 1994, another MOS was established with the IPE, following the launch of its Brent crude futures contract. SIMEX currently offers 12 futures and four option contracts, details of which can be found in Appendix A. The Exchange's fuel oil contract is set for a relaunch in late 1996 or early 1997 following a serious decline in interest. It plans to change the grade of fuel oil listed on the Exchange, to move closer to the bulk of fuel traded on Singapore's cash market.

SIMEX gained much unwanted publicity in early 1995, as the centre that featured in the 'Fall of the House of Barings'. Its performance in the wake of that crisis was very impressive, as it quickly managed to close out the bank's outstanding position, even managing to return some margin payments, and continued to function as before. Since then, preventing a repetition has been a top priority, and an advisory panel was set up for that purpose. All its recommendations were accepted and SIMEX has since become a more closely regulated market.

The Singapore Commodity Exchange is chiefly a rubber market, having three active contracts. There is also a smaller coffee one, launched in 1995, and there are plans to set up metals contracts along the lines of the LME, offering zinc, copper and aluminium. When that happens, a MOS with the LME is possible.

The Hong Kong Futures Exchange (HKFE)

HKFE was established in 1976 as the Hong Kong Commodity Exchange, changing its name in 1985. Its most active contract is the Hang Seng stock index, launched in 1986, with options introduced in 1993. The HKFE uses the SPAN margining system and clears its contracts through its in-house subsidiary. It also renders assistance to the Chinese authorities in their efforts to establish markets within its own borders.

It is generally assumed that the Chinese authorities will allow the free financial markets of Hong Kong to continue after the latter's reversion to Chinese rule in 1997. This is not, however, certain as no announcements have been made; this has created difficulties for the future, causing many companies to make contingency plans in other centres.

The uncertainty has also affected business in the colony, with volumes falling alarmingly. In 1995, HKFE moved its Hang Seng contract onto an automated trading system in an effort to revive interest. Contract specifications are given in Appendix A.

Other Far Eastern exchanges

Of the other Far Eastern centres, Malaysia, the Philippines, Taiwan and Thailand are in varying stages of development. Kuala Lumpur has a commodity exchange where palm oil futures are actively traded. However, the tin, cocoa and rubber contracts are tradeless.

In December 1995, the Kuala Lumpur Options and Financial Futures Exchange (KLOFFE) was established, offering only equity-related products, such as composite index contracts. Financial instruments are set to follow during 1997. All contracts will be on an automated trading system (ATS) and terminals outside Malaysia will be available eventually.

The Malaysian Monetary Exchange (MME) opened for business in Kuala Lumpur in June 1996. Signalling its determination to develop as a regional financial hub to rival Singapore and Hong Kong, it will trade interest rate and currency futures. At the launch, only one contract was listed: three-month Kuala Lumpur Interbank Offered Rate (KLIBOR).

The Manila International Futures Exchange (MIFE) was established in 1991, following the restructuring of the Philippines Commodity Exchange, where contracts are still traded. Options were not traded on this exchange. Unfortunately, it had to be closed down in 1996, amid accusations of price rigging.

Taiwan is the only country that has allowed its citizens to invest in foreign futures markets before the establishment of a domestic futures exchange, which is expected in late 1997. The CME is the most frequently used foreign market. Plans for the launch of a Bangkok financial futures exchange are also tentatively arranged and a commodity exchange is expected to be operational by mid-1998. Probable contracts are rice, rubber, shrimp, sugar and tapioca. South Korea, Indonesia and India are also planning to introduce derivatives trading in 1997. Emerging markets increasingly recognise that if they do not create a market of their own, someone else will step in and trade their products. Indeed, this has already happened in some cases.

China

The Beijing Commodity Exchange trades seven contracts ranging from maize to sodium carbonate. There are now a total of fifteen exchanges throughout the country but foreigners are not yet allowed to trade on any of them. However, the Chinese themselves have made up the deficiency; they are keen gamblers and volumes reflect this.

There are a few financial instruments available – for instance, Shanghai has a Treasury bond market – but an occupational hazard of them all is the possibility of intervention by the authorities to curb trading. They are not, therefore, free markets in the way understood in the West.

The Former Soviet Union and Eastern Europe

The Moscow Financial Futures Exchange began trading in August 1995. It was set up by 14 private-sector Russian banks and aims to become the main centre for foreign exchange trading in Russia. A major drawback of trading in Russia is the possibility of counterparties not honouring their contracts. There are at least three other exchanges, all based in Moscow, trading various commodities and financial instruments but, again, foreigners are not permitted to participate. The St Petersburg Futures Exchange launched a domestic T-Bill contract in 1996 and Kiev plans a sugar market by early 1998.

A wheat futures market was established in Kazakhstan in May 1996. The Czech Republic and Poland are also intending to open derivatives markets within the next year or two, followed, no doubt, by the other East Europe and Former Soviet Union (FSU) countries.

South Africa

Commodity futures trading was launched in Johannesburg in 1995, with contracts for sorghum, soyabeans, sunflower seeds and chilled beef carcasses. White and yellow maize futures were launched in February 1996.

The South African Futures Exchange (SAFEX) offers 24-hour automated trading in stock and gold index contracts, together with krugerrands and bonds. Trading began in 1987 with the index contracts; details of these contracts are given in Appendix A. A traded options market was set up in 1996.

4

Using exchange-traded futures and options

Futures and options markets play a vitally important role in the orderly operation of today's complex financial scene. Their growth since the 1980s has been phenomenal and nowadays, trillions of dollars change hands every day.

In the early days, however, before options were invented, futures trading was a far more sedentary and a less complex affair. Used primarily as a hedging tool, speculation was very low-key and was confined to taking the other side of hedgers' contracts. When trading resumed after the Second World War, the markets quickly blossomed as interest from financial institutions, non-commodity trading companies and, indeed, the general public grew rapidly. Their potential as an investment medium was quickly realised and soon led to the proliferation of contracts that we have today.

Futures markets were developed to provide insurance against price fluctuations. Futures trading is the passing of price risk from one trader to another whose interests are different – one will be fearing a rise in price and the other a fall. The period between the purchase of a commodity at a known price and its disposal at an unknown one (or vice versa) is the period of most risk for a merchant. Volatile price changes amid uncertain communications presented a risk that needed to be hedged if possible. Futures markets provided that opportunity. An advantage these markets have over stocks and shares is the ability to go short (selling without having the goods and hoping to buy back later at a lower price) as well as long, thereby taking advantage of falling markets as well as rising ones.

A futures contract is an agreement to buy or sell a standard quantity of a specified commodity or financial instrument on some specified future date at a price fixed on a recognised futures exchange. The development of futures markets was driven by the underlying supply and demand statistics of the relevant market with both producers and consumers keen to protect themselves against any unforeseen disruptions on the underlying physical markets.

A futures market differs from a forward one because, although physical delivery may be contemplated and is provided for, trading in futures is more like trading in promises. Physical delivery onto the futures market of a commodity in fulfilment of the contract was always implicit and, indeed, it still is. In fact that is seldom the case; with speculators prepared to take the price risk of a hedger's operation, participation ceases long before the contract becomes spot. Making or taking delivery, however, is always possible should it be desired. Financial contracts, on the other hand often specifically call for no physical delivery and cash settlement.

Hedging

The world's first futures exchange was established for the Chicago grain markets, to enable US farmers to hedge their crops safely following a spate of failures and defaults in the mid-19th century. In those days, unscrupulous operators thought nothing of running away from obligations that had turned sour. The CBOT was created, therefore, to protect farmers and other genuine trade operators.

The US wheat farmer could protect himself from a disastrous fall in prices in the period following the harvest by selling an equivalent amount of wheat on the CBOT for delivery the following March or May at the prevailing price. If subsequently the price collapsed, the farmer simply delivered the wheat to the buyer the following March (or May). If the price rose, he could close out his futures position and sell his wheat at the higher price on the spot market. Similarly, a large user of wheat would hedge his obligation in the exact opposite way. In these days of risk avoidance, the buyer and seller often get together to do both the physical and hedging deals at the same time with each other. This is also very prevalent in the sugar market. Nowadays, anything from wheat and sugar to a basket of currencies or equities can be similarly hedged.

Indeed, the original reason for the formulation of futures markets was to provide an inexpensive and secure market-place for producers, merchants and end-users to hedge their operations against adverse price movements caused by the weather, bad and good crops and shipping problems. With speculators taking the other side of these trades and carrying the risk, hedgers are able to lay off any risk that prices will rise or fall from current levels. A hedger views a futures market purely as a vehicle to lay off risk; he is not interested in making a profit. That is for the speculator to seek to achieve.

Here is an example of a simple hedging technique:

A wholesale grocer is duty bound to keep high stock levels of refined sugar to meet his customers demands which have to be satisfied at prevailing prices. Should prices fall in the meantime, therefore, it follows that he has to sell some or all of his stock at a loss. However, if he had hedged his purchase by selling futures against it, any such loss is offset by a profit from the futures transaction. Had prices gone up, on the other hand, his physical profits would have been offset by a futures loss. As he had no way of knowing which way prices would go, he is consequently protected from any sudden price movements and, in theory, comes out all square, as follows:

He buys 500 tonnes of physical refined sugar at, say, $300 per tonne and, at the same time sells the same amount on the futures market, as far ahead as he calculates it will take him to sell the physical sugar. In a perfect world, by the time he has sold his stock both markets would have moved in tandem and he will be able to come out of the transaction at nil profit or loss.

In reality, however, it is not as simple as that as markets seldom move in tandem and there will be a final adjustment to be made. In this example, the wholesaler would, of course, have bought back half the futures position when he had sold half the stock.

Similarly, a producer whether he be a coffee grower or a copper miner, would buy futures to hedge against adverse price movements as he sells his output. Banks are inclined to take a more favourable view of clients who hedge their operations, making it easier for the latter to get more favourable loans, etc. Many trade operators may well have a continual permanent hedge on a market, which would give them stability in the buying or selling of the physical raw materials as well as the flexibility to enhance a hedge by trading just before or just after the physical trade is made. They can also get very favourable treatment in the fields of commissions and margins from their brokers.

Pure hedging operations of this sort are, unfortunately, being made more difficult by the operations of the system and chart traders which tend to distort prices in the short term. This has driven much business away from the markets but has not stopped the trade taking advantage of such distortions, along with others, by using the futures markets more for speculation than for any other purpose. Many genuine hedging operations are now carried out in the currency markets where there are better opportunities and, in any case, foreign exchange risk has become the biggest worry for so many users.

An example of a foreign exchange hedge is the exporter who expects to receive $125 000 from a client in two months' time. He does not want to run the risk of a change in the current value of the dollar, so he sells dollar/sterling futures with a lifetime of two months, thereby offsetting any profit or loss on a dollar movement with a counterbalancing futures operation. Similarly, an importer who has to pay $150 000 four months from now can hedge his position by buying dollar/sterling futures with a four-month life.

Some commodities, such as grain and sugar are often traded in very large quantities like 10 000 tonnes or more. In order to hedge these transactions, it is often necessary to enter into one of the two special operations, known as against actuals (AAs) or execution orders (EOs).

Against actuals (AAs)

AA deals are essentially a straightforward hedge; the difference is that both parties have agreed to the operation, from start to finish, for exactly the same reason a smaller operator hedges his deals. Both sides take opposite action in physicals and futures: the producer sells futures to protect himself from a fall in the price and the consumer buys them against a rise in the price and to safeguard his sales up to the time the physical goods become available, to ensure continuity of supplies to his customers. Once the goods do become available, the futures deals are liquidated at a price acceptable to both parties. The producer delivers the physicals in exchange for the same amount of futures.

The price that the futures side is traded is usually reached by agreement and does not necessarily bear much resemblance to the prices paid on the market on that particular day, since both prices have to be the same to make the operation work and to eliminate any risk from hedge lifting or any unforeseen and sudden price movements. A member of the exchange has to act as intermediary to register the futures transaction on the terminal market. To distinguish the trades from the day-to-day business of the exchange, the letters AA are placed against the deal and this accounts for any discrepancies in the price.

Execution orders (EOs)

EOs are a variation of AA deals but with a higher profile played by the exchange members. Essentially, an AA becomes an EO when each side uses a different broker or trade operator who therefore, has to go on to the open market to set up the futures side of the operation. In this case, the price of the physicals would be the average of the futures selling price for the producer and the average of the futures buying price for the consumer. After the rest of the deal, such as premium or discounts, quantities, shipment period, etc, have been agreed, there might sometimes be a small financial adjustment to be made.

The advantages to the physical operators of a scheme such as this are that they can fix the price of the actual goods at any time they like during the period of the open futures position and, in that way, can benefit from any premium or discounts previously agreed. However, one drawback is that they would be liable for any margin calls that may arise. Physical operators do not have to pay commissions on the futures side of such deals, only the actuals. Brokers can, of course, do simultaneous transactions for both parties; any losses on the futures market would lead to adjustment to the physical invoice. It is a safe hedge.

Arbitrage

Another method of trading futures is arbitrage. Originally this entailed the simultaneous trading of a commodity in two different markets which offered essentially similar specifications but in different currencies. Such deals took advantage of discrepancies in the differentials. This usually needed split-second timing and was therefore available only to floor members. Recently, however, the trend in London and other non US centres has been to alter the basis currency to US dollars, in which most commodities are now quoted, leaving such activities to the currency markets themselves. Probably the only market where such arbitraging is still possible is in London and New York cocoa, where the former still uses sterling – the only London quoted commodity with a fungible counterpart in the US.

Nowadays, arbitraging is defined as the simultaneous purchase and sale of the same commodity in two different markets where absolutely everything is exactly identical; if anything differs, it is not considered an arbitrage. Advantages of such activity, therefore, are somewhat limited. It was, however, exactly this that Mr Leeson was doing in the Nikkei 225 Stock Index, taking advantage of fleeting differences between the Singapore and Osaka, Japan, markets whose contracts were identical. Until things went horribly wrong, it was a very successful exercise. The only difference between these two markets is that Osaka is an electronically traded market while Singapore still uses the traditional open outcry method. The latter method is faster and more transparent and it sometimes took some time for significant market movements to reach Osaka's computer-based operation; this gave astute traders in Singapore with open lines to Osaka the opportunity to take advantage of such delays. Such delays are usually very brief – a few minutes maximum.

Spreading

Arbitraging should not be confused with spreading. A spread position is the simultaneous purchase and sale of two related futures contracts. They do not have to be identical and are used when prices are considered out of line with each other. They can be executed within a single market, i.e. long of the near position and short of a far one, or they can be in two different markets, for example long of Brent crude oil on the International Petroleum Exchange (IPE) and short of light sweet crude oil on The New York Mercantile Exchange (NYMEX). The latter holds far more risk as they can seldom be executed at the same time and often different grades or other specifications are involved.

Spreads can also be performed with different commodities, currencies or securities, for instance soyabean oil and meal on the CBOT or between a three-month US Treasury bill contract and a three-month Eurodollar time-deposit futures contract on the CME. The latter is known as the TED spread.

Other popular spreads are the soyabean crush and the petroleum crack spreads. A crush spread involves a long soyabean position, representing the raw, unprocessed beans, against short positions in oil and meal. The opposite is known as a reverse-crush spread. The petroleum crack spread involves buying crude oil futures and selling the products, heating oil or unleaded gasoline futures.

Trading systems

As mentioned in Chapter 1, until relatively recently, trading in futures was always carried out on exchange trading floors by open outcry. This allows all members of the market to have an equal opportunity to trade, as the dealer who wishes to trade shouts out his bid or offer loud enough for all to hear and the deal is finalised when such bid or offer is accepted by a counterparty. Most markets also have official calls to establish opening and closing price levels. These calls are overseen by an exchange official and are conducted in a formal way with strict procedural rules. An exception to this is the LME where official settlement prices are announced sometime after the close of the morning rings.

Many of the more recently established exchanges do not now have a trading floor; modern technology enables traders to operate from the comfort and security of their own desks via a trading screen which displays the bids and offers and the quantities available at each price, for others to accept or ignore as they wish. Although this method is a lot cheaper to set up and to operate, it removes from the market the eye-to-eye trading and openness of a trading floor.

The over-the-counter (OTC) market is another that offers alternative ways of trading futures but it is totally unregulated and is specially designed to suit the needs of individual customers. Its workings are explained in Chapter 5.

Clearing

All transactions on recognised futures exchanges are settled through a clearing house. Apart from London, most exchanges have set up their own clearing houses as subsidiary companies to settle contracts. London's contracts traded on LIFFE, LME and IPE are settled through the London Clearing House (LCH), a completely separate company owned by a consortium of six UK banks.

The primary role of a clearing house is to act, in relation to its members, as the central counterparty for contracts traded on futures and options exchanges. When a clearing house has registered a trade, it becomes the buyer to the seller and the seller to the buyer of the contract, thus ensuring the financial performance of all trades and guaranteeing their fulfilment. To protect itself against these assumed risks, it sets and enforces minimum standards and establishes margin requirements.

In these days of increasing cross-border and cross-time zones trading, clearing requirements are changing. Already, some exchanges are offering mutual offsetting facilities whereby contracts can be transferred to the clearing house of another exchange and this is likely to expand in the future. As global clearing expands, clients as well as members will be able to have a single point of administrative contact with a consolidated account statement covering all markets. This is already available from some international investment banks.

Market analysis

There are two primary approaches to trading and analysing futures markets – fundamental and technical. Fundamental analysis relies on supply and demand and other physical and factual features, while technical analysis concentrates purely on the price movement of the commodity or financial instrument.

Fundamental analysis

The objective of fundamental analysis is to identify and assimilate the supply and demand factors likely to influence prices and should include other important factors such as the overall state of the world economy and how that might affect the market concerned. Foreign exchange rates and their fluctuations are another important consideration, as is the existence of any international trading policies or commodity agreements that impose export quotas or other conditions that can upset the supply-and-demand balance. Weather conditions in growing areas are a material factor in the grains and tropical foods sectors. Labour relations in mines and refineries in the metals markets, and interest and inflation rates in financial ones are all relevant considerations.

Technical analysis

Technical analysis is quite different; it is the forecasting of future price movements based on the performance of past price action. It seeks to identify certain chart patterns, such as 'head and shoulders', 'double top' or 'double bottom' which provide buy or sell signals. It takes no notice of a market's fundamentals, believing that many of them are, in any case, built into the price before they become common knowledge.

There are nearly as many of these systems as there are traders who operate them, as they all strive to find the perfect system that simply cannot lose. Such a system probably does not exist but, by identifying patterns and trends, these traders can hope to win roughly half the time and so keep in business. Once such a trend is established, often through the use of moving averages or something similar, the amount of interest shown will almost certainly keep it going long enough for the price to go too far, presenting excellent profit-taking opportunities to the quickest. However, to the unconverted, it always seems to take too long for trading signals to be triggered at both ends of the movement, with the result that much of it is missed, along with the opportunity to maximise one's profits. Of course, psychology plays a large part since there are usually many others following the same trend. A drawback of many systems appears to be their inability to take decent profits; so often much of a trend's upsurge is lost before the sell signal arrives.

The basic charting methods are as follows:

- *Bar charts.* This high-low-close chart is the most traditional and widely used method, is simple to construct and easy to understand. The vertical line represents the price range of the day, week or whatever time period is used, the top being the highest price traded and the bottom the lowest. The bar across this line is the closing price. On some charts, this bar only goes to one side of the range line; where there are two of these, the one going to the left indicates the opening level and the one to the right the close.

- *Candlesticks.* These charts are similar to bar charts but concentrate on the relationship between the opening and closing prices. Instead of a vertical line to represent the range, the area between the opening and closing levels is represented by a thin rectangle. If the close is higher than the open, the rectangle is unshaded or white and if the close is lower than the open, it is shaded or black. If the highs or lows are outside this range, they are shown as wicks and if the open and close are both at the same price, a bar across the line indicates that. Interpretation of these charts is complicated as many other things, such as the position of a candle in respect of other bodies, have to be considered. It is a Japanese invention and whole books have been written on the subject. It is explained in greater detail in Chapter 7.

- *Point-and-figure charts.* These concentrate solely on prices traded and are represented by an X if the price is rising and an O if it is falling. Each little square on the graph represents a price, or tick.

- *Moving averages.* These are widely used to identify trends and even to try and spot one before the competition. The objective is to take two of these moving averages (MA) and trade whenever they cross. Choice of averages is up to the individual but 5- and 20-day or 10- and 30-day moving averages are the most common. Alternatively, one of those can be plotted against the closing prices. On a 5- and 20-day moving average, trading signals are generated as follows: a sell signal is given when the 5-day MA falls below the 20-day MA and a buy signalled when it moves above it. Because past prices are needed to construct a moving average, there is a delay before they can catch up; consequently, here again the relevant signal tends to miss a large part of the trend, so the move itself has to be a good one for the exercise to be a real success. For optimum profits, it means that profit taking should not wait for the actual crossing.

Options

Following the 1986 Financial Services Act, all options became fully transferable. Prior to that, they were individual deals between taker and grantor, both of whom had to see the deal through to expiry. Now known as 'traded options', they are 'derivatives' of futures and are the origin of the name derivatives which has now devolved into a multitude of financial activities, some beneficial and some highly speculative.

An option is the right or choice – but not the obligation – for the payment of a premium, to buy or sell a futures contract at some agreed time in the future which can, in theory, be years ahead. Most deals, however, are for a far shorter period of time. There are two principal types of options – calls and puts. If the investor thinks the market is going up, he buys a call option and, if down, a put option. The taker of the option pays a premium to the grantor and stands to lose only that amount, whatever the market does. His profits, on the other hand, can be unlimited. The grantor keeps the premium and if the taker abandons the option (i.e. the market fails to move in the right direction by more than the premium) it becomes a straight profit. However, if the market does move in the right direction by more than the premium, the taker will exercise the option, meaning that the grantor has to honour the other side. It is prudent, therefore, if granting calls, to have the currency, stock or commodity ready for delivery. Otherwise, it may be necessary to cover in a sharply moving market, leading to substantial losses.

For example – An investor wishes to buy silver as he thinks the price will go up. The price of silver three months ahead is $5 per ounce, so he purchases a call option to buy 100 000 ounces in ninety days' time at $5.05 per ounce. If the price of silver does not exceed $5.05 after ninety days, the investor abandons the option to pay $5 for the silver, losing his 5 cents premium, a total of just $5000. However, if the price had risen to, say, $5.25 per ounce during the period, the investor would exercise his option to buy his 100 000 ounces at $5 per ounce and immediately selling it for $5.25, a profit of $20 per ounce (the difference between $5 and $5.25 less the 5 cents premium). So by risking $5000, the investor made $20 000.

It is also possible to trade in double options, i.e. a call *and* a put (usually for double the premium). Exercise of the call causes the put to expire unexercised and vice versa. Double options are often used in commodity trading and they also have an important part to play in OTC financial modules. The advantage of buying options as opposed to futures is the limit placed on a possible loss; that loss cannot exceed the premium paid at the outset, while profits are limitless. All risk management programmes are dependent upon options in one form or another.

Options were originally started in the Chicago grain markets in the early 1930s. By 1934, however, the abuse of them became so widespread that they were prohibited by the US federal government and it was not until the early 1970s that trading resumed. The catalyst was the freeing of the dollar causing the value of currencies to fluctuate daily. Options traders have the added advantage of not having to pay margins as they do not have an open position. They provide much needed liquidity to a market and, to go back to the example, have the leverage to control $500 000 for only $5000, a leverage of 100:1.

There are three types of option – European, American and Bermudan; the difference between them lies, in exercising them. European-style options have a fixed exercise date that can only be implemented at maturity, while an American-style option has a floating date, enabling the holder to exercise it at any time. The Bermuda-style option is somewhere in between and can be exercised on a number of pre-determined dates as stated in the contract. After the exercise date, all options are worthless.

Since 1986, when options become fully transferable under the UK Financial Services Act, the growth of options trading has been phenomenal; in the case of currencies much of it has been on the OTC market where it largely consists of one-off, specially tailored options for individual clients. For that reason, it is impossible to quantify the growth rate effectively; suffice it to say, it has grown from almost zero to trillions of dollars per day in the ten years to 1996. The fantastic growth of traded options is largely due to the expansion of the OTC market and its amazing range of exotic options. The ingenuity of providers of financial modules based on currency and equity options has spawned an endless array of esoteric names for them. From All-or-Nothing Options to Zero Strike Price Options, there are literally hundreds of them, with more being invented all the time (see Appendix E).

Events in foreign currency markets tend to trigger the rapid growth of exotic options, which are mostly designed by investment banks and are largely confined to currencies, although both equity and interest rate markets have their fair share. Commodity options tend to remain the straightforward traditional types, sometimes known as 'plain vanilla' options. The increasing uncertainty and volatility of foreign exchange markets together with the likelihood of a single European currency have instilled caution into the activities of many users.

Among the most popular exotic options are Average Rate Options, the settlement of which involves an average exchange rate rather than a high one, and Basket Options, in which a number of currencies are included and which rely on a correlation between them at settlement.

By far the most widely used exotic is a Barrier, or Trigger, Option which has several basic variations to it. It has become an especially popular tool for the management of foreign exchange risk. There are four basic types – calls and puts, each with either a knock-out or knock-in feature. The barrier is a pre-determined exchange rate level which, if reached, is activated by the knock-in feature or killed by the knock-out feature.

Because of their uncertain life, these options tend to be cheaper than the more conventional ones. Other variations of a Barrier Option are a reverse knock-in one and a 'range binary' which is a derivative of a Binary, or All-or-Nothing Option and can be used as a trading or hedging instrument. A list of the more common exotic options is given in Appendix E.

Inventors of exotic options are often likened to rocket scientists in the minds of people outside the industry. To get a proper grasp of the business takes years of study as well as a degree in mathematics.

Options can be 'in the money', 'out of the money', or 'at the money'. A call option is in the money if the market price of the underlying instrument is higher than the strike price, whereas it is out of the money if the market price is lower than the strike price. For put options, the reverse is the case for both. An option is at the money when the market and strike prices are the same.

Ordinary options are guaranteed by a clearing house in the same way as futures; in the case of OTC exotics, however, that is not the case – the grantor, usually a bank, takes the other side onto his book and takes all the risk.

A wide range of models is used in pricing options, the best known of which is the Black–Scholes method. Most of them take the same basic variables to determine the price, including the underlying physical price, the option strike price, the risk-free rate of return, the time to expiration and the historic and implied volatilities.

Funds

The desire of investors to have a broad coverage of commodity or financial futures without the cost of separate positions in them, led to the advent of futures and options funds. These funds present the opportunity for investors to spread their risks. They work in exactly the same way as unit trusts or share investment funds on the Stock Exchange. In addition, most of them provide a built-in guarantee that losses will be limited to the investor's original stake. Each fund has its own rules and usually guarantees that, if the portfolio falls to a certain level, the fund is liquidated and the remaining cash repaid to the investors. It is a truism to say that for every commodity that is falling in price, there is another that is rising, so a good comprehensive coverage of the markets should prevent fund liquidation. Investment in these funds reduces risk but it also reduces rewards by limiting the profits.

The sheer weight of this these investments can briefly distort prices as counterparties either disappear or retreat rapidly, hoping for a better price.

This has had the effect of driving away many of the traditional users of futures markets. It has become increasingly difficult on some markets to put on a satisfactory hedge when prices are fluctuating widely owing to speculative activity. This is proving counter-productive as many traditional users are forced to look elsewhere for their hedging operations.

An exception to the tendency towards reduced risk but limited profits are the so-called hedge funds – a misnomer if ever there was one, as one thing they do not do is hedge – which are highly geared, highly speculative funds designed to take a short-term position in a market, relying on their own size to move a market and thus enabling a quick profit to be made. This sometimes works but more often does not, although profits on the successes usually outweigh the losses on the failures.

Hedge funds were a product of the 1980s and one problem with them was their sheer size. The amount of money invested by them in a market was often too much for it, causing gross distortions to the price. This back-fired on to the funds themselves as, as soon as the buying stopped, prices fell back to their correct levels. This made profit-taking extremely difficult, if not impossible, as the same thing happened the other way. This has led to smaller hedge funds and greater market liquidity. For further treatment of funds see Chapter 6.

5

OTC derivatives

OTC or 'over-the-counter' derivatives are bilateral transactions that are privately negotiated and settled off-exchange. Derivatives are by definition 'derived from something else'. They can be derived from ('written on') any underlying instrument or asset, provided that a valuation of that underlying instrument can be agreed by the two parties to the contract. This means that the underlying asset must be some form of homogeneous product where a publicly observable market exists. Most commonly, OTC derivatives are written on interest rates and foreign exchange. Large markets also exist for OTC contracts on equities and commodities. More recently, markets have begun to develop for derivatives on credit and insurance risks.

OTC derivatives are used for hedging and taking risk. Because they are derived from an underlying asset and their price moves in relation to that asset, they can be used both to immunise (hedge) risk to that underlying or to gain exposure to it. That is, they can be used to offset financial risk arising from price changes in the underlying asset, or they can also be used to create financial risk.

OTC interest rate and foreign exchange products

OTC derivatives come in two basic forms – swaps and options. There are, of course, a huge variety of derivatives within these two basic forms but they will all be either deterministic (swaps) or contingent (options). Below are outlines of a few of the most frequently used products.

Swaps

The most common deterministic OTC derivatives are swaps. A swap is a contract where two parties agree to exchange different pre-determined cashflow obligations. These cashflows can be in the same currency or in two, or more, currencies. An interest rate swap (IRS) is an exchange of cashflows in a single currency. It is called an 'interest rate' swap because the two parties to the contract are typically exchanging interest flows of a different basis in the same currency – fixed for floating, for example. In fact, the source of the cashflows that the two parties decide to exchange need not be an interest rate flow, but they could be cashflows from a variety of sources.

Swaps are traded in all major markets and currencies. The largest, most developed market is in US dollars (US$) followed by yen and the major European currencies. There are also large markets in the currencies of all major developed countries, and of a number of developing countries.

Interest rate swaps

The fixed-for-floating IRS is probably the most frequently traded OTC derivative. The two parties to an IRS (counterparties A and B) exchange cashflow streams described as either pre-determined amounts or referenced calculations, to be paid on pre-specified dates. Normally, at the time of entering into the swap the present value of the cashflows to be paid will be equal to the value of the cashflows to be received – it is, after all, a swap. (This is from a theoretical perspective – in practice there will be a small net difference in value between the two streams which will reflect the market maker's bid–offer spread.)

A typical IRS will be an exchange of a fixed interest rate for a floating or variable rate. OTC contracts can be customised to fit any requirement, but a typical US$-based swap contract might be an exchange of a series of fixed semi-annual payments for a series of variable semi-annual payments indexed to an agreed reference benchmark – most typically LIBOR (London Interbank Offered Rate, i.e. the rate that banks lend to each other in the interbank or wholesale market). The swap will have a pre-agreed term (maturity) and size. For example, a three-year, US$100 million, fixed-for-floating IRS would involve party A agreeing to pay to party B a fixed interest rate of, say, 6% on a semi-annual basis for the next three years on a principal amount of US$100 million. In exchange, B will pay to A the six-month US LIBOR rate, reset and paid semi-annually, for three years and on a principal amount of US$100 million (Fig. 5.1). The principal amount, the underlying size of the contract, is more correctly known as the 'notional principal' on an IRS – it is the reference amount used to calculate the cash interest payments due but is not itself exchanged.

For readers new to financial markets an understanding of interest rate swaps may be made clearer by considering a familiar example. If a company takes out a loan from a bank or finance company it will be for an agreed amount, for an agreed period (term) and at an agreed rate of interest. Typi-cally, the agreed rate on loans is a floating interest rate which is regularly reset to reflect changes in market interest rates. This is because most banks finance themselves through deposits or interbank wholesale funds which are themselves indexed to short-term interest rates. The bank lends at a margin above its own cost of funds. Prior to the advent of swaps and other OTC derivatives, a bank would typically lend on the same basis as it raised funds so it could avoid exposure to interest rate movements. For a company borrowing money to finance, for example, the building of a new factory, it is vital to know the cost of the borrowing (interest rate) in order to calcu-late the viability of the investment. If the borrowing is linked to a variable rate, the company runs the risk that over the life of the loan, interest rates

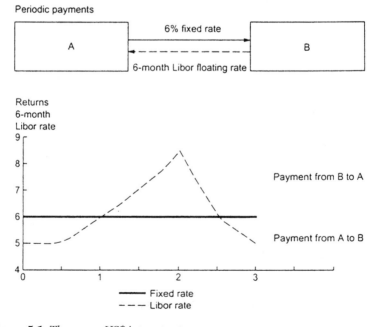

Figure 5.1 *Three-year US$ interest rate swap.*

may rise to such an extent that the investment would no longer be economically viable. For example, if a company invested in a project which was expected to provide a return of 10% when short-term interest rates were 4% – and then saw rates rise to 10%, the project would become uneconomic. To solve this problem the company could enter into an IRS to cover (hedge) the loan. Under the IRS, company A in the example would agree to pay a fixed rate of interest in exchange for having the variable interest rate due on its loan paid for it by B. In this example, the company might agree to pay 6% on a three-year US$100 million IRS (matching the term of its loan) and receive LIBOR payments – the LIBOR payments would be paid to the bank to service the loan. Thus, in essence, the company has obtained a loan at a fixed interest rate and can be certain that its cost of financing (6%) will remain below the 10% return on the investment.

The pricing of swaps

The pricing of swaps and other interest rate derivatives reflects the market pricing for short-term interest rates in the future. The fixed-rate leg of a swap will thereby have a present value equal to the sum of the present values of the anticipated short-term rates. For short-term swaps (typically up to two years) in many markets these future LIBOR rates can be implied from listed money market futures (e.g. Eurodollar contracts). On longer-dated swaps the forward rates (future short-term rates) must be implied from the fixed rate of the swap. The fixed-rate leg of a swap can be seen as the 'predicted' average cost of the offsetting variable rates at the time the contract is written.

As mentioned above, at the time of entering into a swap the net present value is zero. The passage of time and changes in market interest rates will result in changes to the net value of the contract. This is also important when looking at the market exposure of a swap. A common fallacy is the assumption that the notional principal of the swap is indicative of what is at risk. In the current environment of derivative scares this often causes alarm. The notional principal is in fact the reference amount upon which the interest payments due are calculated, while the value at risk is the current difference in value of the two offsetting cashflow streams (replacement cost), plus any anticipated further deviation in value depending on future movements up until maturity. This is typically somewhere between 5% and 10% of the notional principal on a medium-term swap.

Cross-currency swaps

A cross-currency swap (CCS) is an exchange of interest and principal pay-

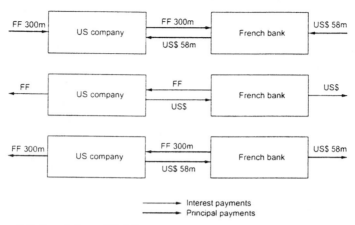

Figure 5.2 *French franc/US dollar cross-currency swap.*

ments in different currencies. The parties to a CCS typically swap cashflow obligations in two currencies, although swaps involving three or more currencies are possible. An example of a CCS might involve a major American corporation borrowing French francs and then entering into a CCS with a French bank to exchange the francs obligation for a US$ obligation. A standard CCS differs radically from an IRS because the principals in the two currencies will be exchanged at both the start and end of the swap transaction. The value at risk is thereby increased as the net present value of the transaction over its life will be additionally affected by movements in the exchange rate of the swapped currencies.

Typically, the principal amounts are exchanged at the start date of the transaction at the prevailing spot rate. Interest payments calculated on the principal amounts are exchanged periodically and, at maturity, the principal amounts are re-exchanged at the same spot rate (Fig. 5.2).

FRAs

A forward-rate agreement (FRA) is a single-period interest-rate swap. An FRA fixes, or hedges, LIBOR for a single reset period. It is quoted as a fixed rate for the desired period and then a single payment is made when the floating side (LIBOR) is set and the difference is calculated. FRAs are very widely used in large volumes by banks to hedge interest rate mismatches on their assets and liabilities. They are priced in the same way as interest rate swaps.

OTC options

Options or contingent products provide exposure where the payout is 'contingent' on some event occurring. The payout is contingent because it only occurs if, for example, the price of the underlying exceeds a certain threshold (strike price). Some of the earliest types of OTC option were simple puts and calls on equities. A typical call option on the price of an equity will logically only be exercised if the price of the equity is higher than the strike price during the exercise period, because the owner or holder of the option can exercise the option – i.e. purchase the equity at the pre-agreed strike price and, theoretically, sell it in the market at the current, higher, price thus realising a profit. The most frequently used types of options include the following.

Foreign exchange options

Foreign exchange (FX) options are contracts to buy or sell currencies at pre-determined rates. An FX option provides the holder with the right – but not the obligation – to purchase an amount of one currency with another currency at a pre-determined spot rate (strike price) for which a premium will have been paid. Most typically, currency options are European style (one exercise date) but Bermudan (a series of exercise dates) or American (exercise any date up to maturity) are also common.

Many variations to the basic structure are available, the purpose of these being either to reduce the cost of the option or, more exactly, to meet specific hedging goals. Common variations include *knock-out* options – in which, if the underlying spot rate moves outside a pre-specified range, the option expires early – and *knock-in*, where the underlying spot rate must reach some pre-agreed level before the option becomes live. These types of options are also called *barrier* options. Barrier options are popular as a way to reduce the cost of buying options, particularly where the buyer has a clear view on future market movements. *Binary* (also called digital) options are those in which the payout is discontinuous – a single (large) payment is made if the underlying breaches the strike price, unrelated to how far into the money it moves. The OTC market for FX options is substantially bigger than the listed exchange market as the flexibility of structure allows exact matching of a client's hedging or investment needs.

Caps/floors

Caps and floors are conceptually simple products. They are akin to insurance contracts that protect the buyer from interest rates rising above a pre-agreed level (in the case of a cap) or falling below a pre-set level (a floor). The purchaser of a cap pays a premium upfront to the seller which requires the latter to compensate for any rise in interest obligations above a pre-set level (the strike). The cap will be referenced to a market interest rate, most typically LIBOR. The mechanics of the product are that the writer of the cap will make payments to the buyer, if and when rates rise above the strike, of the difference between the reference interest rate and the strike.

Consider a UK-based company purchasing some new machinery which is funded by borrowing £10 million. Assume the machinery will provide an acceptable positive return if interest costs remain below 9%. Assuming short-term (three-month) sterling interest rates are 6.125%, the company could purchase an 8% cap at a cost of 2.7% upfront. This would ensure that the borrowing cost is never more than 8% and will be lower if LIBOR remains below 8%. The additional cost of the cap, which adds approximately 0.8% per annum to the cost, would maintain the total borrowing cost below the requisite 9% (Fig. 5.3). A floor works in the same way except that it protects the buyer against rates falling; thus an investor can purchase a floor to lock in a minimum interest level on an investment.

A cap or floor is often an alternative to a swap as both achieve a similar aim in providing hedges to interest rate costs. The pricing of caps and floors depends (as with swaps) on the current level of interest rates and, additionally, on the level of interest rate volatility. A cap or floor is an option on interest rates – it only pays out if the underlying (interest rate)

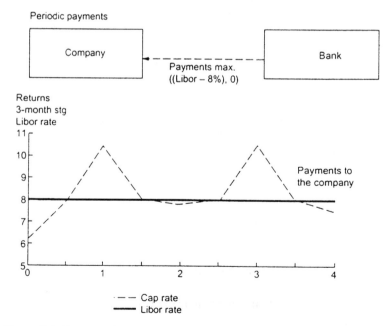

Figure 5.3 *Four-year interest rate cap.*

reaches the strike level. The level of volatility will determine how likely it is that the cap will pay out and how much it will pay. Higher volatility implies a greater likelihood that rates will move enough to break the strike. The higher the volatility, the more valuable the option is and the higher the premium will be.

A very popular product is a combination of a cap and a floor – called a *corridor* or *collar*. The simultaneous purchase of a cap (a ceiling, as it were) and sale of a floor provides a maximum and minimum rate of interest (therefore a corridor). The sale of the floor, depending on the strike, will partly or fully finance the cost of the cap. By entering into a corridor the buyer is giving up some of the advantage of lower interest rates to reduce the overall cost of the hedge.

Bond options

Options on bonds, both basic puts and calls and more exotic varieties such as 'spread' and 'quanto', are widely used.

A *spread* option allows a risk position to be hedged or established on the relative performance of two different assets – the spread between them. Thus a spread option between two bonds – US Treasury bond yield minus German Bund yield, for example – would give an investor exposure to US Treasuries outperforming Bunds without taking a view on the absolute direction of overall bond markets. Spread derivatives are, of course, available on a wide range of other underlyings.

Quanto derivatives index the payout to a currency different from the currency denomination of the underlying. For example, a UK investor may believe that Deutschmark (DM) bonds are going to rise, but does not have a view (or may be negative) on the DM against sterling (stg). The investor could therefore buy a DM bond call option quantoed into stg. The 'quanto' element fixes the payoff in stg terms; thus, if the investor's view is right, the payout in stg will duly reflect this.

The OTC market tends to complement the listed bond futures option market in Government bonds, allowing for customisation to suit an investor's preferences. OTC contracts are also used for transactions on corporate and Euro bonds.

Other OTC derivatives

Commodity derivatives

A well-developed OTC derivative market exists for certain commodities, most notably crude oil and oil-related products (heating/fuel oil, gas, etc). The largest market is for crude indexed to either WTI or Brent as a pricing benchmark. The reason that the market has developed more rapidly in crude oil than in other commodities is that oil best fits the requirements for a derivative market. It is liquid in the financial sense, with a large volume of trade in the underlying physical market which is itself of a huge size. It is relatively homogenous, and it is widely used by, and its price has a major impact on, a large number of businesses, governments, etc. This means there is a large demand for hedging/exposure to oil prices. As a comparison the smaller and less-developed derivative market for aluminium is characterised by fewer numbers of potential 'players' – organisations with exposure to financial risk due to aluminium price movements – and a considerably smaller overall physical market. The most common OTC contracts on commodities are swaps and simple options.

Equity derivatives

A full range of OTC derivative products (swaps, options, exotic options, etc) is traded on equities. OTC equity derivatives are traded on single stocks, baskets of stocks and indices.

Baskets of stocks can be single-sector baskets – UK utilities, for example – or more specific customised groups that fit an individual counterparty's requirements. An investor might, for example, want to purchase an option providing upside exposure to the performance of Boeing, British Aerospace and Daimler Benz, with the return hedged into stg.

Index transactions probably account for the largest single sector of the OTC equity derivatives market, the most popular indices being the major market indices – Dow Jones, S&P 500, FTSE 100 and Nikkei 225.

Equity derivatives are widely used to provide retail investment products such as stock indexed deposits where an investor enjoys a percentage of the upside performance of a stock market and is guaranteed the return of the capital at maturity.

Uses of OTC derivatives

OTC derivatives are used to transform existing asset or liability risk profiles or to create new risk profiles. The great flexibility of OTC products allows virtually any financial exposure to be reduced or enhanced. Regular uses include the following:

● Hedging financial risk exposure to underlying price risk

- Modifying existing asset or liability cashflow structures
- Reducing the cost of borrowing
- Enhancing the return on investments
- Accessing new markets for sources of capital
- Exploiting competitive advantages
- Corporate finance activities

The following are examples of some of these broad uses in specific applications.

Hedging financial risk

Manufacturing companies are exposed to a variety of financial risks, many of which are hedgeable with OTC derivatives. Hedgeable risks often include:

- Foreign exchange (FX) risk
- Interest rate risk
- Commodity price risk

FX risk will come from overseas sales of products invoiced in foreign currencies. A machine tool manufacturer in the UK exporting to France will be exposed to the FX risk of income receipts in French francs (FF) against a cost base primarily in stg. This may be complicated further by cost implications of raw materials billable in US$. In order to protect profitability, the company can enter into forward FX sales of FF for stg. However, the company may often choose to purchase FX options if it is unsure of the volumes of its sales to France, as it will not want to be committed to sell FF in the future if it fails to make sales and therefore has no FF to sell. To reduce the cost of these FF/stg FX options it might add a layer of customisation, with a knock-out feature linked to the US$ against stg rates. The rationale would be that a fall in the US$ would mean cheaper raw materials, thus indirectly compensating for any fall in the FF.

Additionally, the firm may want to hedge its raw material costs by purchasing options or entering into swaps on gas or oil prices and metal prices. Again, by judicious customisation and looking at the overall financial risk profile of the company, costs of the hedging products can be reduced.

If the company is borrowing to expand its capacity, it should hedge the interest rate risk on its borrowings so they are consistent with the income the new productive assets are expected to generate. In the case of a manufacturing company that will typically mean entering into an interest rate swap to lock in a fixed cost of borrowing.

Modifying cashflow structures

Swaps, particularly, are very useful for restructuring cashflows to match financial requirements more closely. This might be, for example, to bring asset and liability cashflows more into line, so as to reduce borrowing or reinvestment risks.

A lender which is extending fixed-rate mortgage loans to its clients will have a mismatch with the liability side of its balance sheet, where it is funding these loans through retail deposits on which it is paying short-term (variable) rates of interest. In order to hedge the exposure of the fixed-rate mortgages the lender will enter into interest rate swaps where it will exchange the fixed-rate receipts for floating-rate receipts, which will match up with the floating rates on the deposits.

Swaps can also be used to modify the maturity profiles of asset on liability flows. An insurance company anticipating a growing volume of claims (payouts) in future years but which has a large volume of receipts (inflows) in the near term on coupon-bearing assets could enter into swaps whereby it makes payments in the early years and receives a large balloon payment at the maturity of the swap. It is thereby locking in the reinvestment rate on its receivables.

Reducing borrowing costs

The swap market is said to have been born in the early 1980s as a tool for reducing borrowing costs. One of the first currency swaps is claimed to have been between the World Bank and IBM, in 1981, in order for both parties to reduce interest rate costs (classic arbitrage). In this transaction, IBM had raised money in Swiss francs (SF) and the World Bank in US$; they then entered into a currency swap which had the net result of providing the World Bank with SF at a cheaper rate than if they had borrowed direct, and IBM with the same in US$. The reason that such a cost saving could be achieved was that both borrowers were unfamiliar names in the respective market in which they raised funds. Thus IBM could raise very attractive funds in SF because the company had been unavailable to SF investors before this time, whereas the World Bank had been a frequent borrower. This is also an example of using swaps to access fresh sources of capital.

Corporate finance activities

Derivatives enable corporations to manage a variety of corporate activities better by limiting financial risk. These activities include takeovers, mergers and competitive tenders.

A company hoping to make a takeover bid is, *inter alia*, exposed to the share price of the target company. Depending on the bid situation, it might want to purchase put options on the target company's stock to hedge purchases of the target's shares. If it is concerned that, having purchased a large block of the target – and with the share price high because of market anticipation of the takeover, the takeover may not succeed, this will limit potential losses. Using OTC products also carries the obvious additional advantage of being private. Such usage must be analysed carefully to avoid any breaches of regulations such as insider trading rules.

In a competitive tender for a contract to build a power station a company may use options to hedge interest rate, FX or other exposure that would result from winning the contract.

Market participants

Market makers

The main providers of OTC derivatives are major international commercial and investment banks and financial product subsidiaries of certain big insurance companies. OTC derivatives are generally provided alongside other wholesale financial services as part of the firm's capital market operations. The largest and most successful market makers in OTC derivatives typically have large market-making capacity in the underlying products.

Sovereign governments

National governments and state agencies are big users of OTC derivatives. They are, almost exclusively, users of swaps and options to hedge the cost of foreign currency borrowing.

Many national governments need to fund a portion of their borrowing requirements in the international market. Governments such as Sweden, Belgium, Finland and New Zealand have been big borrowers in overseas markets, raising foreign currency debt. Sovereigns utilise OTC derivatives to minimise interest costs and to try to manage foreign currency exposure to match foreign trade flows or currency baskets.

State agencies are also big borrowers on international markets. Export credit agencies, national power corporations, etc, will borrow in markets which provide the cheapest relative cost of funds and then use swaps to convert the liability into their local currency or that which matches their assets/income flows.

Banks

Banks are the largest single category of users of OTC derivatives for their own internal purposes exclusive of any market-making activity they may provide. The size of bank balance sheets and the interest rate and currency exposure within them make the use of derivatives essential.

Corporates

A very sizeable percentage of large companies use OTC derivatives, the most widely used products being FRAs and FX options.

The credit risk inherent in transacting OTC derivatives means that only relatively large companies are able to use them. Furthermore, OTC derivatives are 'wholesale' market products – the usual minimum size of an interest rate swap is US$5 million equivalent – again determining the suitability of the product for larger organisations only.

Market size

Given that OTC derivatives are private contractual agreements, it has always been a problem to gain a clear picture of the size of the market. An insight was given by a survey published by the Bank for International Settlements (BIS) in conjunction with 26 central banks which estimated that as of 31 March 1995 the global OTC derivatives market had $47 trillion in outstandings. A more recent estimate is given in Table 5.1.

Another insight was given by the BIS estimated daily turnover of OTC derivatives. This had global turnover of interest rate swaps at US$63 billion per day and turnover of interest rate options as US$21 billion per day (data compiled during April 1995).

Table 5.1 *Estimated size of the global OTC derivatives market at 31 Dec each year (in $ trillion)*

	1996	1995	1994	1993	1992	1991	1990
Interest rate swaps	26.1	19.5	14.6	9.9	7.4	5.9	4.4
Interest rate options	5.8	4.4	3.4	2.9	1.8	1.6	1.5
FRAs	4.2	3.9	3.8	2.7	2.5	-	-
Currency swaps	2.1	1.8	1.5	1.3	1.2	1.2	0.8
Currency options	2.3	1.9	1.5	1.1	1.1	-	-
Currency forwards	12.3	10.8	11.5	9.2	8.1	-	-
Other OTC derivatives	1.3	0.9	0.6	0.3	0.2	-	-
Total	54.1	43.2	36.9	27.4	22.3	-	-

Source: Swaps Monitor, NY, NY. Estimates of contract outstandings.

Risk management of OTC derivatives

Both market makers and users of OTC derivatives need to have appropriate risk management procedures and organisation in place. The major risks that require managing are explained in the following sections.

Market risk

Derivatives provide leveraged exposure to the price risk of the underlying instruments. Close monitoring of the amount and types of risk being assumed is therefore paramount, as is a full understanding of the mechanism of any derivative products traded. The management of an institution also needs to have a clear policy on the use of derivatives (e.g. for hedging or for trading of risk).

Credit risk

The performance of OTC contracts is dependent on the creditworthiness (ability to pay) of the counterparties to the contract. Users of derivatives need to monitor the credit quality of the counterparties with whom they have derivative exposure on an ongoing basis. Exposure must be monitored to include both current marked-to-market (MTM) value and potential future exposure (due to anticipated market movements).

Operational risk

OTC derivatives are often the most complex type of financial transactions that a company enters into. The operational infrastructure of the firm needs to be able to cope with, *inter alia*, the regular valuation and settlement of derivative contracts.

Legal risk

OTC contracts are stand-alone bilateral contracts and must be drawn up in a legally unambiguous form. They are often traded across legal jurisdictions. Most OTC business is now transacted under a standardised set of documentation developed by the International Swap & Derivative Association (ISDA). Most contracts are executed under an ISDA Master Agreement that permits cross-product netting (to reduce credit exposure). Netting means that one can look at the net exposure of all contracts with another counterparty, on the basis that in the event of bankruptcy only the net value is at risk.

An example

A major market maker of OTC derivatives will have a portfolio of tens of thousands of contracts totalling hundreds of billions of dollars of notional principal equivalent.

The OTC derivative department will typically be split into desks based on the underlying products, such as interest rate derivatives, FX derivatives, equity derivatives, etc. The department will contain traders (managing the product books), marketers and deal structurers.

There will be a separate, independent, risk control department reporting directly to senior managment, responsible for analysing the market risk taken by the trading desk and calculating the firm's risk of loss (typically called VAR – Value at Risk) on the positions being run.

A separate credit risk department will perform the same function for risk of that kind and will be responsible for authorising counterparties as suitable to trade with and determining appropriate line limits (the amount of business that can be written with the particular counterparty).

The financial accounting and the settlement of contract undertaken by the derivatives trading desks will be managed by a separate accounts and settlements department.

It is vital to isolate the different functions so that suitable independence and control of the business exists.

Conclusion

Since the mid-1980s, the growth of OTC derivatives has been one of the key elements in transforming the financial markets. Linked to the growth of cheap computational power on the desktop provided by PCs and computer workstations, complex and customised transactions can now rapidly be developed, priced, analysed and managed. Virtually any financial risk can be priced and therefore hedged or entered into. OTC derivatives provide bridges between markets, allowing risks to be priced and transferred.

Despite some of the well-publicised teething troubles of what is still a relatively new market, OTC derivatives are now well established and very widely used by the majority of participants in many wholesale financial markets around the world. New markets for OTC derivatives are beginning to develop for hedging credit risk (via default swaps and options) and insurance risk.

Currently there is much focus on the credit exposure resulting from the structure of the market, where transactions are undertaken bilaterally between parties. There is growing use of MTM collateral agreements between parties to reduce mutual exposures. Credit derivatives are also beginning to be used, to manage credit exposures by either offsetting credit risk through default options or exchanging credit risks via credit swaps. The next logical step is some form of clearing house which would enable unique customised transactions to continue to be booked and allow credit risk and collateral to be agrregrated.

The flexibility that OTC derivatives provide to tailor transactions exactly to specific risk requirements has resulted in the rapid growth of the OTC market and will ensure its continued development.

6

Managed futures

In this chapter we will look at managed futures – the use of futures and options as investment tools in their own right. In this regard the managed futures industry is unique because it is derivative fund management in a pure sense, using futures and options in their own right in managed accounts or collective investment schemes.

Background

Many economists might well claim that John Maynard Keynes was the first professional managed futures trader. The world-renowned economist took advantage of the commodity markets and the application of a disciplined trading approach. He studied commodity fundamentals and made substantial returns on his investments. However, the American trader Richard Donchian, who may well have been the inventor of the 5-day and 20-day moving average, is generally recognised to be the father of the managed futures industry. What Donchian did was to apply the disciplines of risk management and control together with the application of a technical, and therefore dispassionate, approach to market trading in the first managed futures fund. Donchian's initial trading back in the 1940s has blossomed into the 2500-plus Commodity Trading Advisers (CTA) currently registered with the US Commodity Futures Trading Commission (CFTC) in Washington. Today in the UK, the regulator of the futures industry, the

Securities and Futures Authority (SFA), also recognises professional traders and has recently designated them as Derivative Fund Managers (DFMs).

Trading futures and options in their own right in order to make a return on an investment is fundamentally different from using them to alter the risk/reward profile of an underlying asset. The little research that is available tends to demonstrate that about 83% of all private clients trading the futures and options market on a speculative basis lose their money. The reason for this is not hard to find. Futures trading allows participants to short sell something that they do not own in order to buy it back at an anticipated lower price – and to leverage (these concepts have been explained more fully elsewhere). Most trades by non-professionals are normally under-capitalised, over-leveraged, under-researched, not properly protected, and represent the adage of 'hope triumphing over experience'. As most of us know, it usually does not. This cavalier process was observed by many of the more aware brokers in American wire houses. Rather than see their clients trade themselves into oblivion, some quickly recognised that the preservation of client equity and its future growth would in the long term provide a far greater return for both client and company than a short-term high commission-to-equity ratio, which is almost always the signal of a forthcoming financial obituary notice.

The more astute brokers started to recognise also that the application of structured trading approaches, together with protection of equity, would simultaneously reduce subjectivity in trading and increase market protection of capital. Some of these brokers observed that, once trends in markets are established, they have a tendency to continue over time. If these trends can be discovered early on and then leveraged, substantial returns can be achieved. Thus was born the technical trend-follower, making money by following the maxim 'trend is your friend', an approach still in use today by the majority of professional managers in the managed futures industry, who now use various forms of sophisticated technical trend-following styles.

Most of these early pioneers were employed in the various brokerage houses. As a consequence, a natural conflict of interest arose. The primary remuneration of the brokerage house was commission generated. Yet it was obvious that high commission-to-equity ratios were a major cause of client losses, and the growth of the managed account was firmly pushing the industry from brokerage return into fund management longevity. This resulted in the creation of specific fund management operations within many of the houses which would, over time, develop an independence more akin to traditional fund management in fixed income and equity markets.

Market observations

There are some historic lessons to be learned from the growth of the managed futures industry. In particular, it has been noticeable over the years that the industry normally does well during periods of volatility and that the returns, when analysed and compared with traditional returns from stocks, bonds, property or other assets, are what is referred to as 'non-correlated'. What is meant by this is that the return obtained from a managed futures account which may be trading a range of commodities and financial instruments may have no relationship to that of an equity or bond portfolio. This was particularly true in the early days of the industry when most of the trading was carried out in the commodity markets. The other important factor, already mentioned, is the ability to go short. In particular, the short positions held by a number of managed futures traders at the time of the stock market crash were perhaps a catalyst in shifting industry attention from the almost exclusively retail side that it had created for itself up until then towards institutional players, who started to recognise the positive portfolio impact that managed futures might have (Table 6.1).

Table 6.1 *Performance of managed futures against US and international stocks and bonds, 1986–95*

Year	Managed futures[1] (%)	US stocks[2] (%)	US bonds[3] (%)	Int'l stocks[4] (%)	Int'l bonds[5] (%)
1986	3.8	18.7	15.6	40.2	11.2
1987	57.3	5.3	2.3	−3.4	7.7
1988	21.8	16.6	7.6	32.0	7.1
1989	1.8	31.7	14.2	20.0	2.5
1990	21.0	−3.1	8.3	−31.0	4.6
1991	3.7	30.5	16.1	6.8	14.2
1992	−0.9	7.6	7.6	−8.0	13.0
1993	10.4	10.1	11.1	27.2	17.5
1994	−0.7	1.3	−3.5	−3.4	−3.3
1995	14.4	37.6	19.2	7.7	16.1

Notes:
[1] Barclay CTA Index
[2] S&P 500 Index
[3] Lehman Brothers Government/Corporate Bond Index
[4] EAFE Index
[5] Salomon Brothers Non-dollar World Index
Source: Managed Futures Association

Results support theory

The basis of modern portfolio theory – for which economists have won Nobel Prizes – can be summed up as follows: 'don't put all your eggs in one basket'. This is not as frivolous as it may sound. For, in fact, the research work of Dr Harry Markowitz and others demonstrated that, if a portfolio was made up of a variety of underlying assets with non-correlated or negatively correlated returns (Table 6.2), then the overall risk/reward ratio or efficiency of that portfolio could be improved (Table 6.3).

There are trade-offs between the level of return investors are seeking against the level of risk they are prepared to take. By adding managed futures to a traditional portfolio made up of stocks and bonds, it is possible to increase the absolute return of the portfolio. This is something which is intuitive and based on the use of leverage. However, what is perhaps not intuitive and therefore more startling is that the application of this higher return and supposedly higher risk investment (managed futures) can reduce the total risk of the existing portfolio because of the non-correlated nature of the returns achieved in managed futures (Table 6.3).

In straightforward language, if equity markets are going up, down or sideways, there may be very little relationship to what currency, interest rates or commodity markets are doing. A detailed study taking Markowitz's initial work and applying it to managed futures, was originally carried out by Professor Lintner of Harvard University and

Table **6.2** *Managed futures are non-correlated with stocks and bonds over the short term*

| | Correlation of monthly returns | | |
	Stocks	Bonds	Managed futures
Stocks	1.000		
Bonds	0.337	1.000	
Managed futures	0.072	0.099	1.000

Source: Managed Futures Association

Table **6.3** *Managed futures diversify stock portfolios to benefit investors on a return–risk basis*

Managed futures in portfolio	Average annual return (%)	Standard deviation (%)	Return–risk ratio
All stocks	14.9	13.9	1.1
10%	14.9	12.0	1.2
20%	14.8	10.6	1.4
30%	14.6	9.5	1.5

Source: Managed Futures Association

subsequently expanded upon by Dr Morton Barratz, Almer Orr, Dr Scot Irwin, Martin J Gruber and Gerald C Rentzler and others. The most recent study – and perhaps the broadest to date – by Dr Tom Schneiweiss, undertaken on behalf of the European Managed Futures Association (EMFA), was published in March 1996. What most of these studies have tended to demonstrate is that by including managed futures within a traditional portfolio of stocks and bonds, the overall efficiency of that portfolio can be improved by increasing its return and reducing its total risk.

Having briefly examined history and significance of managed futures, we will look at some of the players, products and structures that are available.

The professional managers

The term Commodity Trading Adviser (CTA) is a historic one enshrined in US statute. However, it is today somewhat misleading, as CTAs primarily trade financial futures rather than commodities and they have discretion over the trades, rather than providing third-party advice. However, the term CTA is unlikely to be changed. In the United Kingdom, where the industry is younger, the Futures and Options Association, working together with the SFA, has come up with the more relevant term Derivative Fund Manager (DFM). (At one point these were to be referred to as Derivative Investment Manager but the acronym DIM was considered somewhat pejorative.) Most of these managers today are regulated by either the CFTC in the United States, the SFA in the United Kingdom or the COB in Paris. While there are other regulators around the world, many DFMs and CTAs register with the CFTC as a matter of choice to obtain market regulation and status. The growth of regulation and control primarily emanates from the United States, and the modern CTA has to provide monthly reports and returns across all accounts and funds to the regulatory authority. All CTAs must produce what is referred to as a *risk disclosure document*, which is something between a marketing document and a statistical abstract of their historical performance.

Trading styles

There are many approaches to trading markets, and entire books have been written about different trading styles. Jack Schwager's *Market Wizards* and *New Market Wizards* are not only great fun to read but also cover a broad range of DFMs. While there is, however, no magic formula that can be applied, there are some general observations that are worth mentioning.

Most DFMs apply technical as opposed to fundamental analysis of markets. What is meant by this is that they analyse a variety of historical price and other statistical information about markets and then apply a structured or systematic form of analysis to predict future movements. This is based on the concept that, while the past may not predict the future, it may indicate its probable course. The most popular form of technical trading is *trend following*, which in its simplest form will follow established trends and only close out positions when the trend has clearly ended by having broken down past some support level.

Fundamental traders, on the other hand, will try and accumulate extensive economic information about a particular market, using historic prices, demand and supply, seasonal information, government policies, commodity pricing supports, exchange rates, and so forth. From this wealth of data and their own knowledge and experience they will then make investment decisions.

The criticisms that are often levelled against each approach may be summarised briefly as follows.

Technical

No matter how objective the approach, subjective decisions have to be made to determine what to include, what to exclude and how to weight the different inputs. Other concerns relate to the following conundrum. If you update your trading approach to changing market circumstances, how can you honestly know if the past track record is relevant to the current one if your approach has dramatically altered? If, on the other hand, you do not change your approach then how can you know if it is still valid if underlying market conditions have dramatically changed?

Fundamental

The obvious problem with fundamental trading can be dependence on a star trader who may move from one DFM/CTA to another. The other difficulty is that you cannot possibly analyse all fundamental information. And even if you could, how could you know what is important and what is not?

The elusive quest for the true trading method seems to lie somewhere in between. Many managers in fact use both technical and fundamental factors when looking at markets. The common factors that seem most relevant to success – irrespective of style – are hard work and discipline, leading to a consistent risk-adjusted track record over time.

The Commodity Pool Operator
(CPO or Manager of Managers)

This somewhat unusual concept is relatively unique to the managed futures industry. The Commodity Pool Operator or 'Manager of Managers' is normally a professional who will structure portfolios made up of managed accounts or funds, thus combining the performance of a variety of external CTAs or DFMs. The CPO thereby aims to create an optimum return by the judicious study of correlations between CTAs and the diversification of methodological approaches and assets managed. This is similar to the Markowitz concept of the efficient market hypothesis, extended to the micro level within managed futures. For example, if the best five performing managers of the previous year were all currency specialists, and if all of them used various forms of trend-following approaches then, by structuring a portfolio based on those managers, future returns might be substantial during years when they get it right, but could be poor (because of the highly correlated nature of those returns) if they all simultaneously get it wrong. Consequently, a CPO who knows the job may combine different styles, such as technical trading with discretionary trading, arbitrage, option strategies, neural networks, etc, together with a broad range of underlying assets in order to ensure genuine diversification within the portfolio.

Over the years a symbiotic relationship has developed between the CTAs and the CPOs, with the CPOs providing distribution and seed capital – particularly in the early years of the industry – and CTAs providing ever-hoped-for returns. Today, however, this division is not as clear as it used to be. Many CPOs are developing in-house CTA capabilities, and many CTAs are developing their own funds and CPO-like operations.

Managed futures information

There are a number of trade magazines (e.g. *Managed Account Reports, Futures and Options World, Futures Magazine*) and statistical analysis firms (e.g. TASS, Barclay) which provide detailed scrutiny, analysis and commentary on the performance of the professional managers in the managed futures industry.

Managed futures terminology

It is beyond the scope of this chapter to cover all aspects of the terms used in the managed futures industry, but a working knowledge of some of them will be useful. This industry, similar to the computer industry, uses terminology peculiar to itself. Most of the terms relate to risk reward measurements. The most commonly used are as follows:

- *Drawdown* – a euphemism for losses. The current loss on an open futures position. It is not strictly speaking a loss until the position is closed out.
- *Margin to equity* – amount of margin monies needed to cover open traded positions.
- *Roundturns per million* – number of roundturns (buy and sell or sell and buy) future transactions opened and closed during one year for each $1 million under management.
- *Standard deviation* – a measure of volatility of returns. The standard deviation measures the average spread of monthly returns around the mean – the lower the better.
- *Percentage rate of return* – average return or loss over a specified time period.
- *Sharpe Ratio* – a risk/return measure qualifying, in a single number, the relationship between return and risk by removing the risk-free rate of return. Usually expressed as:

$$\text{Sharpe Ratio} = \frac{\text{average monthly return} - \text{risk-free rate}}{\text{standard deviation}}$$

The higher the Sharpe Ratio, the better the performance.

Remuneration

Remuneration in the managed futures industry is, by traditional fund management standards, quite high. The CTAs normally receive a management fee which can range from 0.3%, and a performance fee which can vary between 10% and 30%. Typically, the performance fee is only paid on net new gains. Some CTAs will base their fees on the absolute return of the portfolio while others will only charge on the value added return of the portfolio. The value added return is the return after the risk-free rate, normally the treasury bill rate, has been deducted from the total return earned from investing in the market. Without addressing all the arguments about whether these fees are justified or not, they have essentially been driven by retail market forces in the sense that, historically, they originated from the retail broking side and were accepted without much question. As the managed futures industry has tried to develop institutional business, the fees have started to come in line with more traditional fund management and are normally expressed in basis points rather than percentage points.

Structures

There are two primary ways of taking up managed futures as a means of investment. One is via a managed account and the other is via a fund. In the last few years a number of hybrid products have been developed in which managed futures have been wrapped inside insurance bonds, commodities, equities and other securitised products.

The managed account

'Managed account' means exactly what it says: it is a direct agreement between the manager and the client. There is a minimum sum required to open the account which can vary from manager to manager and can be as little as $10 000 in some cases, but more typically would range from $0.25m to $1m. Some of the larger managers will not accept managed accounts below $5m. The terms and conditions of the managed account are normally disclosed in a risk disclosure document, but can be negotiated directly between the manager and the investor. The investor's broker will receive a daily report, called an equity run covering all positions traded and probably showing the bottom-line performance of the account. The manager will also issue monthly trading reports and returns.

Funds

Funds or collective investment schemes are as common in the managed futures industry as they are in the traditional fund management industry. In the United States, because of regulatory restrictions on the use of futures and options within mutual funds, the major vehicle has become the limited partnership. In the United Kingdom in recent years, specific regulations have allowed for the creation of unit trusts which trade primarily futures and options. Overall, the regulatory restrictions of the onshore structures have led to the growth of the industry offshore. Outside the

United States, one of the reasons for this is that the nature of the investment is perhaps more sophisticated than traditional investments and, as such, the more sophisticated investor will be aware of and possibly less concerned about comparative levels of protection versus costs and can work out on his own the benefits of onshore versus offshore investment vehicles.

In most cases when investing in a collective scheme, this is usually set up in some sort of fund, with reports and unit pricing on a monthly basis, normally without transparency as regards the individual transactions that the CTA is undertaking. The primary advantage of investing via the fund route is limited liability together with a lower entry level. Typically, many funds will accept investments from as little as $1000, and in almost every case significantly below the normal minimums for a managed account.

The guaranteed fund

The very attraction of the managed futures investment – projected high returns which are non-correlated to traditional assets – is simultaneously one of its greatest weaknesses. The reason is quite simple. Higher returns by definition must be associated with higher risk, not just in managed futures but in all investments. If the returns do not materialise, what is the value of non-correlation? Hence the idea of guaranteeing the initial value of the investment. That means returning to the investor after a pre-determined period of time the amount of money that he or she originally placed, thus providing a level of assurance that would not otherwise have been available and which, in its absence, may well have prevented the investment in the first place.

The original concept of the guaranteed fund worked particularly well during periods of high interest rates. The yield curve would normally reveal the return over time that could be achieved. This might be created via a deposit, a gold swap or a US Treasury Zero Coupon Bond. This 'safe' return would be locked in over time and the original capital would be assured. For example, if annual interest rates were, say, 10% and the investment was $1000, then on a compounded basis $621 could be placed on deposit and after five years return the original $1000 investment. Meanwhile the balance of $379 could be used for the futures and options trades. Normally these structures would have to be put together in such a way that if more than the amount available for futures trading ($379) was lost, then the guarantor, be it a CPO or a third party, would underwrite any further losses in order to keep the integrity of the guarantee intact. These guaranteed funds work extremely well from a marketing standpoint, in the sense that they remove the objection of unknown risk. Their weakness is that the cost of the guarantee (particularly as interest rates decline) tends to dilute the return. Also the opportunity cost of the guarantee (alternative uses of the non-trading money) has become apparent to a number of investors who realise that the 'real' return can only be made from trading the underlying markets. Having said that, the guarantee structure had – and continues to have – a very important role within the retail market as it helps remove many of the obstacles, primarily based on fear and ignorance, that would otherwise prevent investors from going into the managed futures industry at all.

More complex guarantee structures

In order to overcome the limitations of these simple guarantees, a number of financial institutions – Citibank being a leading one – have structured marked-to-market guarantees whereby the period of the guarantee is shortened to increase market acceptance and the guarantee requirements are marked-to-market on a daily basis, which can allow greater flexibility in the amount of money available for trading the underlying markets. Other guarantee-like structures have also been developed. These include the use of guaranteed bonds whereby the coupon of the bond is less than the norm, and this portion is used for the leveraged trade, with the managed futures component itself wrapped up inside the bond. The advantage of this type of approach is that the bond is a known and acceptable vehicle, and a discounted coupon may be significantly enhanced by the managed futures return over time. This has been seen to be an attractive way of promoting a managed futures investment.

Measuring returns

Because of the diverse nature of the trading styles and the double alpha effect – that is, CTAs can go long and short – it has been difficult to determine a single benchmark against which the industry can be measured. This has unquestionably proved a handicap because the bulk of the institutional investors tend to be peer driven and benchmark oriented. In practice they need to be able to measure performance. The managed futures industry has made a number of valiant attempts to create a variety of benchmarks, but the problem has been mostly related to the fact that a relatively small industry ($25 billion) has created a plethora of benchmarks. These include benchmarks on individual CTAs, benchmarks on pools, benchmarks on guaranteed funds and non-guaranteed funds, benchmarks on specialist areas, etc. Consequently, up to and including today, most people look at the industry as an absolute return industry and will measure return against a risk-free rate of return which they could achieve by placing funds into some form of riskless debt instrument or even cash. This approach has not proven totally satisfactory and there is continuing discussion and investigation in order to create an acceptable benchmark for third parties to apply when assessing the returns they achieve from a managed futures investment.

7

Market analysis

There are literally thousands of different trading strategies for derivatives, and every self-respecting fund manager has their own preferences and, very often, their own exclusive pet theories. This is not, therefore, the place to expand in any great detail but it is important to get some idea about the range and complexity of the more widely available schemes that are on offer.

Many of the more modern strategies are designed to manage and contain risk rather than to go for capital growth but, arguably, it can be said that for every risk management strategy, there is a speculative scheme on the other side of the deal. High-profile failures such as Barings and Orange County gave the industry a bad name but they certainly curbed some of the excesses that were creeping into the system. Risk management programmes got a higher profile as companies reconsidered their strategies, and the days of sitting back waiting for profits to come in from activities that directors did not understand – and whose potential dangers they did not appreciate – were over.

Nevertheless, however low derivatives may be in the public's esteem, the fact remains that the extent to which they are being used has never been greater. From fixed-interest mortgages to index-linked savings accounts, they play an integral and indispensable part in the risk management strategies of fund managers.

As explained in an earlier chapter, there are two basic trading methods: fundamental and technical. An overwhelming majority of trading strategies follow the latter method, which can be described in a nutshell as predicting future price movement from past performance. Sophisticated refinement of the basic charting methods described in Chapter 4 form the basis of these strategies.

Charts are used to analyse the price prospects of a market. The basic technique was invented in the USA by Charles Dow of Dow-Jones, although Japanese candlestick techniques are far older. Many professional investors use charts as a valuable source of extra information, utilising them in conjunction with fundamentals. Others ignore fundamentals completely, considering them a hindrance that serves only to confuse the issue.

The Elliott Wave and the Quantum theories

There are many commercial companies, particularly in the USA, offering various methods and ways to improve investment performance. One of the best known and more successful of these is the Elliott Wave theory, invented by R N Elliott between the two World Wars. Derived from observations of stock market behaviour, Elliott brought together a set of principles that applied to all degrees of wave movement in the stock price averages. Through meticulous study he uncovered the organisational principle behind the movement of markets. The basis of his theory is that a bull market has five waves, three up and two downward corrections. The bear market that follows has three waves, two down with an upward correction in between. That completes the cycle and the next bull market is set to begin. These cycles are allied to time periods which can be anything between a day and 200 years. Elliott identified nine different time periods and he also set out a series of rules concerning the relationships of different waves. As he grew more proficient, his accuracy improved significantly.

The theory is now widely followed by many investors. Those who use it agree that it is a good general framework to follow but many feel that it needs to be combined with other tools to create new hybrids for better results.

Elliott himself was constantly hoping to improve his theories and introduced the Fibonacci numbers into the system. Leonardo Fibonacci was a 13th century Italian mathematician who discovered the unique number sequence that bears his name. He claimed that this sequence and its ratios are present throughout the natural world. The Fibonacci sequence starts with 2 and continues by adding the preceding number: thus the sequence runs 2, 3, 5, 8, 13, 21, 34, 55, 89 and so on. The ratio between successive numbers is 1.618 or (inversely) 0.618 and between alternate numbers is 2.618 (0.382). These ratios are used to calculate price objectives for the waves.

Another widely followed theorist is William D. Gann, a market trader turned 'guru'. He also studied market waves and ratios, and his Quantum theory concluded that moves of 25%, 50% and 100% were common, while moves of one-third and two-thirds also occurred, though less frequently. His ratios are based on the relationship between the extent of a price movement and the time it takes to achieve it.

These two systems form the basis of many a fund manager's trading strategy and they are particularly useful in setting price targets and corrections. There are several books on these subjects for those who wish to study the theories in greater detail.

Candlesticks

Japanese traders started using charts centuries before they were used in the West. 'Candlesticks' are now very popular and enjoy a wide following. They are a sort of up-market high, low, close bar chart with added sophistications.

The body of a candlestick is a box drawn between the opening and closing prices for the period. If the close is above the opening price, the body is unshaded or white, and if the other way round, it is shaded or black. The former indicates a bullish range, the latter a bearish one. The line, or wick, above and/or below the body is known as the *shadow*; this represents the difference between the open and close and the high and low prices for the period. The shadow location indicates the strength of the buying or selling: above the body, it indicates buyers lacked the strength to sustain new highs and below, the opposite is indicated. The length of the shadow indicates how the market reacts to price levels: the longer the shadow, the greater the potential rejection of the extremes of price by the market's participants.

Japanese charting techniques are becoming very popular as more and more people study them; kagi, three-line break and renko charts are just three of the many methods available for study. Kagi charts highlight trend strength support, resistance and congestion areas, and indicate when to offset positions originally placed with candle signals. Three-line break charts plot price action independently of time; they highlight trend direction and signal reversals, and provide an analysis method for closing-price-only markets, such as fixed income yields or unit trusts. A renko chart is similar to a three-line break chart except that its chart lines are all exactly the same size, while break charts vary in length.

Other technical indicators

Another technical indicator is Bollinger Bands, which are trading bands that vary in distance from the moving average as a function of a market's volatility. They are used to determine over-bought and over-sold levels, to locate possible reversal areas, to confirm divergences and to project price targets for future market moves.

Others include stochastic oscillators, sequential analysis, regression lines and relative strength indices. There are hundreds of others, many of them under copyright. A useful source for these techniques is *Futures Magazine*, a US monthly publication. It is also possible to buy specially tailored off-the-peg computerised trading systems; prices range from under $100 to tens of thousands of dollars. The software concerned, however, is most likely to have the actual system hidden from the purchaser – referred to as black-box or canned systems.

For the smaller speculator and beginners, the best strategy to adopt is probably that of trend following. This is very popular and, as one gets more experienced, it can be refined, diversified or altered in any way to suit the individual. Trend following is probably – if properly and carefully disciplined – the easiest and most painless way to make (or lose) money. However, the investor can expect considerable opposition as it is indeed very popular. To stay ahead of the competition, therefore, it is necessary to have that little bit extra, as prices can quickly become distorted by moving too far too fast. To judge this crowd movement, there are techniques available, allied to moving averages that can signal advance warnings of trend subsidence. Moving averages are, in effect, a variant of a trend line although they are calculated mathematically rather than drawn straight onto the chart. The shorter the period of the average, the more closely it tracks the price. Five-and 10-day moving averages are widely used and anything over 20 days presents too delayed a picture.

In order to have that little bit extra to stay ahead of the competition, many investors turn to indicators that give early warning of a price movement. Some of these indicators measure the speed at which a market is moving. Known as *momentum indicators*, or *oscillators*, they are used to identify short-term turning points. They work best in a sideways-moving market, detecting the speed at which price has been moving and thereby giving early warning of a break-out and the establishment of a new trend line. Another popular indicator is the Relative Strength Indicator (RSI). This detects when a market is over-bought or over-sold; when a market reaches either of these states, the reversal will be all the more violent and so these call for early profit-taking where possible.

A drawback of many of these technical systems is the difficulty of being able to spot the optimum time to take profits; by the time the signal arrives, much of the movement has been reversed and the profit lost. To a committed fundamentalist, this seems to be a major flaw. There are many books on the manifold strategies but, in most of them, it appears that it is not possible to maximise profits satisfactorily.

Neural networks

The trading strategy that can consistently beat the market has yet to be invented but it is claimed that neural networks – or artificial intelligence as it is sometimes called – comes close. This system, which aims to replicate human thought, tries not only to copy the thought processes of the world's finest brains but also to improve upon them.

Unlike other trading systems, neural networks do not have rules; they look for patterns, just as human thought does. Humans learn from these patterns and quickly change direction, but other systems cannot do that. However, patterns for neural networks can only be formulated through the data given to them, such as supply-and-demand statistics, price history, technical indicators etc, from which they endeavour to follow human thought processes through to a successful (and profitable) conclusion.

Some might think that human thought is the biggest drawback to successful program trading, as the urge to tinker with a system in mid-flow is often too strong for some people to resist. Many trading systems fail to achieve their full potential for one of two reasons: first, altering the inputs into a system in contravention of its rules is nearly always fatal and, second, the system is unable to signal the taking of a profit early enough to ensure an acceptable return. It is this second problem that neural networks seek to rectify.

A neural network is initially trained to handle a specific problem, such as forecasting the price movements of a currency. Like teaching a small child to read, many of the replies are gibberish at first but they are corrected by the training process until they become more accurate. When a neural network makes a wrong guess, an adjustment occurs, strengthening the right track connections and weakening the wrong ones. As in all trading systems, good and bad signals have to be identified and dealt with. In some commercially available programs in the USA, the network is created and trained by the program itself and all the client has to do is to provide the example data to produce the required result. All this sounds extremely complicated, and it is. It is this that gives the derivatives industry its aura of superior and incomprehensible theories which prompt remarks about a degree in rocket science being needed to understand them. Indeed, the principles of rocket engine turbulence were used by one former rocket scientist to market a system in the USA.

The basic presumption of a neural network system is that meaningful patterns exist in the movements of derivative prices. These patterns are quickly identified so that users can input these to their advantage, in anticipation of the next patterns. The systems act as tools to search through vast amounts of data in order to detect these patterns. They can do this far quicker than humans and, although computer based, they do not need active programming of the search techniques by users as the process is completely automatic and based on trial and error. One advantage of neural networks is their ability to spot relationships that would otherwise be missed; all markets are subject to speculative bubbles which have little to do with the available fundamental data, and these bubbles can be compensated for. Neural networks can also be trained to spot relationships between different markets such as stock and commodity indices.

Neural networks are not considered by many investors to be as satisfying as exotic options but they are becoming more and more heavily marketed and are considered a useful supporting tool in some quarters.

Exotic options

Exotic options have been covered briefly in another chapter. These are largely OTC tools, specifically tailored for individual clients to suit their own needs by banks or large investors who take the risk onto their own book. A list, with explanations, of the most common of these exotic options is given in Appendix E.

Fundamental analysis

Few traders rely solely on fundamentals for their trading strategies; indeed, many ignore them completely. In financial markets where the only fundamental of consequence is the economies of the G7 countries, this is particularly so. However, fundamental analysis has the advantage of always being correct in the sense that the supply-and-demand situation determines the prices in the long run – it is just the timing that can be awry, owing to the machinations of the technical traders.

Forecasting accurately the supply-and-demand situation of commodities has been made a lot easier by the fall of communism. Hitherto, figures from former communist countries included a high element of guesswork, especially for metals. Although still by no means *completely* reliable, figures from those countries are now far more reliable and can be more accurately incorporated into the global picture.

There are many agencies and brokers that issue supply-and-demand figures, some more reliable than others, but there are many other factors to consider in assessing the fundamental position of a commodity. These include weather patterns, acts of God, political events and decisions, stocks, shipping capacity, substitutions and price sensitivity. Fundamentals affecting each commodity are quite different and each needs to be assessed according to its own peculiarities.

Adverse weather conditions, for instance, in the plains of the USA will severely affect the grains crop and, similarly, the cocoa crop will suffer from bad weather in West Africa and/or Brazil. Sugar, on the other hand, being a far more global crop, is not so affected by weather. It is important to be aware of weather conditions in key areas, and there are several good specialised agencies which provide such a service.

Seasonality plays an important part in successful fundamental analysis. A knowledge of the seasonal cycle that affects agricultural commodity prices, such as the lows that usually coincide with harvesting, is essential. The price patterns appearing on charts also attract technical traders to seasonality considerations, giving added emphasis to them. In financial markets, regularly scheduled government statistical information can also noticeably affect bond and currency prices, and Treasury bond futures are often weak at the beginning of the US tax year. Annual weather changes affect heating oil prices.

Acts of God, such as hurricanes, earthquakes and volcanic eruptions, often have a significant impact upon markets. These can sometimes have a long-lasting effect since both earthquakes and volcanic eruptions can have a delayed effect on weather in areas thousands of miles from the starting point and can also disrupt weather patterns for up to a year after the event.

Political events and decisions are always difficult to predict, not least because they can be quite irrational on occasions. It is easy to get caught out by a sudden change of policy which is not easy to cater for. At times of low prices, politically motivated alliances between producing countries try to withhold supplies from the market. This always pushes prices up but how long such an alliance lasts depends entirely on the trustworthiness of the participants. An example of a successful alliance is the coffee producers of Latin America, who successfully limited supplies following the collapse of the International Coffee Agreement. An unsuccessful example is OPEC (the Organisation of Petroleum Exporting Countries), where export quotas are routinely ignored by all the signatories.

Stock levels are always an important consideration in a fundamental scenario and it is essential to know what they are. While it is not difficult to find these out, they can be fragmented and not give a complete picture, so it pays to check this. Stock/consumption ratios are very useful tools and are sometimes even used by technical traders.

Some commodities are more price sensitive than others but nearly all have a ceiling somewhere – even coffee encountered strong resistance from the public at its peak in the late 1970s. Where circumstances push prices to very high levels, it is only natural to search for or change to a cheaper alternative. This often has considerable cost implications and is not, therefore, always viable unless it is certain that the alteration will remain cheaper for a considerable time. However, copper and aluminium, for example, are interchangeable in some uses and price plays an important part. Similarly, if soya meal becomes too expensive, farmers will look elsewhere for their cattle feed. Rubber is at risk from synthetics and sugar from artificial sweeteners. The latter are considerably more expensive than sugar but the health lobby can be very vociferous.

Finally, fluctuating exchange rates can affect one's calculations. Wild gyrations thankfully seem to be a thing of the past, but any sudden movement in the rate of the US dollar against another major currency can sometimes make nonsense of one's careful analysis of a commodity. A knowledge of the economic prospects of the leading industrialised countries is, therefore, also necessary. Exchange rate risk can easily be hedged on the currency markets.

Translating the general principles of fundamental analysis into sound working assessments is a painstaking job but one that should bring its rewards. Statistical techniques such as regression analysis are very useful and are widely employed. Such exercises are more effective for longer-term timescales and are definitely not for the short-term or day trades.

Regulation and management

CHAPTER

8

Lessons from the past

In a market where a one-eighth movement in interest rates or a hundredth of a point in an exchange rate can bring massive rewards to those on the right side of the transaction, unscrupulous operators are bound to appear. The very complexity of derivatives adds impetus to their machinations. This complexity is very often aided and abetted by deliberate obfuscation on the part of many participants, particularly on the Over-the-Counter (OTC) market.

Futures markets were first formed in the mid-nineteenth century specifically to counter fraudulent activity on the spot and forward markets where, at that time, defaults were quite commonplace when prices moved adversely. In the 1980s and 1990s, up until the Barings crisis, the ignorance of supervision and the total lack of controls over rogue traders caused many spectacular frauds, some of which were even perpetuated and abetted by the very supervisors who should have prevented them. The monetary rewards available were too much for some people and the pursuit of Mammon transcended all else in the quest to keep the profits coming.

There will always be lessons to be learned from the past, the Barings collapse in 1995 being a case in point. If nothing else came of it, it certainly concentrated the minds of everyone concerned, particularly the industry associations. It was incomprehensible that millions of pounds could be sent every day to an overseas office without any questions being asked by head office management. Compliance and supervisory procedures have been tightened up everywhere since then.

Examples of fraudulent trading

History is littered with episodes of fraudulent dealings; perhaps the oldest instance is the Great Tulip Crash of 1637. From the mid-16th century, following the introduction of the tulip from Turkey, kings and princes in Europe imported and cultivated them. The creation of the Dutch tulip industry can be traced back to this era; the plants were ideally suited to the climate there and, by the 1620s, with demand rising steadily, there were many different varieties and colours.

By 1636, everyone was dealing in tulip bulbs, and regular markets had been established in Amsterdam, Rotterdam and other towns in Holland. Prices continued to rise and many people grew very rich. 'A gold bait hung temptingly out before the people, and one after the other, they rushed to the tulip-marts, like flies around a honeypot,' wrote Charles Mackay in *Extraordinary Popular Delusions and the Madness of Crowds* in 1841 (reprinted in 1996, Wiley Investment Classics). Everyone imagined that the passion for tulips would last for ever; markets flourished in Paris and London and many foreigners were smitten by the frenzy. Houses changed hands for two or three tulip bulbs, the prices of which reached 5500 florins (c. £4100 today) for the best ones. Then, suddenly, soon after another dramatic increase in prices, a dealer found he could not re-sell a bulb. It was February 1637 and the dealer's predicament, combined with the excessive credit generated by the rush, caused a panic. Everybody tried to sell at once and the price fell from 4000 florins to 300 in a matter of days. By April, the price was down to 35 florins and many were ruined.

Excessive credit was the downfall of the tulip bulb industry and exactly the same thing happened again in London in 1720 when the South Sea Company collapsed. By the beginning of the 18th century, the English economy was exceptionally sound, backed by the Bank of England and other great chartered corporations. A growing favourable trade balance encouraged commerce, industry and agriculture, but there was little control of credit. Many leaders of industry felt that the country's resources were not being properly utilised and that even greater prosperity could be achieved if they were.

The directors of the South Sea Company decided to try to do something about this. The company had little to do with the South Seas – the name was simply a front. Its main function was financial – as a rival, almost, of the Bank of England. The intention was for the company to take over a large portion of the national debt at a fixed-interest rate and use its credit to finance capital expansion. The directors became greedy for riches and ignored all prudent safeguards; they even bribed politicians with stock. Deplorable methods were used to inflate the share price, and the situation got out of hand. As speculation mounted, many people borrowed money and pledged their possessions to become even more heavily involved, thinking the price would rise for ever. When the inevitable crash came, many became bankrupt and destitute and the very foundations of government were severely shaken.

The tin crisis

Both these scams hold important lessons for today and there are many parallels to be found in recent events. Nothing goes up in price for ever. Prominent among recent examples is the tin crisis of 1985 when, on 24 October, the International Tin Council (a United Nations body with 23 sovereign states among its members and, at the time, without question the largest tin trader in the world) announced it could no longer meet its financial obligations and could not pay for the contracts that were due to be delivered that day. The banks refused to give the ITC's buffer stock manager (BSM) any further credit lines.

For some months previously, the ITC, through its BSM, had single-handedly bought up all the tin on offer, both physically and on the LME, each day paying a higher price than the day before, to keep the price up. By the time of the default, the price had been artificially pushed to an unprecedented £10 000 per tonne. Unfortunately, the BSM did not have the funds to do this unaided but, by availing himself of the various legitimate methods of borrowing, rolling forward and gearing in the market – in addition to promising commission business to those ring-dealing members who helped him – he was able to acquire the necessary credit.

At this time, the BSM only had to report his stock levels six months in arrears, so the ITC had no idea of the true situation. There were also other ways he could cloud the issue, for instance through unpriced forward sales. These sales officially allowed him to deduct that tonnage from his stock but, since they had no fixed price, when the price fell, his realised sale price dropped accordingly. Consequently, the real stock position was far, far greater than that officially announced. Other methods were 'special lends' and 'special borrows'. In the former he reduced his stockpile by selling spot metal to a merchant at a fixed price and simultaneously buying the same quantity for forward delivery at the same price – the forward long position would not be counted as part of his stock until actually delivered. These deals were tantamount to borrowing money to finance stock but structured to bypass his officially authorised bank borrowings. This illegal, though self-perpetuating, scheme would last as long as the interest payments were kept up and firms continued to believe that the situation would last for ever.

'Special borrows' enabled the BSM to keep the price up without using his own money to buy the surplus stock. He arranged with a counterparty to buy spot and sell forward tin at the same time. This kept the spot price firm without utilising bank borrowings or ITC funds. The only cost was the interest paid to the counterparty. All this goes to show how easy it is, especially if backed by a highly respectable institution or company, to acquire the necessary finance to perpetrate a massive fraud. When the inevitable crash came, the extent of the operation was found to have cost £900 million – more than the sum that brought down Barings Bank. The total was spread among several different merchants, brokers and ring-dealing members but was, nevertheless, extremely painful to many of them.

This episode had serious repercussions on the entire industry and prevented the resumption of tin trading on the LME for several years; the LME itself had to be completely reorganised. Trading was finally resumed in 1990.

As is always the case, much heart-searching followed, controls were tightened up and trader supervision intensified. Nevertheless, that did not stop similar things happening again; the 1980s are littered with such episodes – Prudential-Bache, LHW, Bankers Trust and Salomon Brothers, to mention just a few. Some of these were caused by over-zealous traders frantically trying to keep up commission earnings and to protect their own jobs. Lack of responsible supervision, however, greatly affected the companies' reputations.

Recent events

The 1990s, too, have had their fair share of scares: rogue traders at Barings, Daiwa and Sumitomo, misguided trading strategies at Metallgesellschaft and Orange County, churning at Gibson Greetings and by cold-calling bandits in offshore centres.

The huge losses incurred at Barings and Daiwa banks were made by traders who were totally unsupervised and allowed to carry on unhindered, and who compounded the losses in desperate and unsuccessful attempts to rectify their positions. Although trading in different markets, the guilty rogue traders in both banks were in control of their own clearing and settlement procedures, enabling them to hide their dealings until the loses became too great to continue to do so. A similar situation prevailed at Codelco, the Chilean state-owned copper company, when a rogue copper futures trader made losses of around $200 million through unauthorised trading on the LME in 1993/4.

In 1996, a rogue trader at Sumitomo – who was allowed to operate unchecked for a decade – was finally unmasked, having managed to hide over $2 billion losses trading copper on the LME. In fact he was making huge profits by manipulating the market tended to cloud the judgement of his superiors; it was a similar situation at Barings.

In the early 1990s, Metallgesellschaft (MG), Germany's leading metals trading company, made an ill-considered investment in a small US oil refinery which soon needed more and more money to be pumped in to make it viable. MG initially entered into a processing deal under which it would sell crude oil to the refinery and buy back its refined production. In order to protect its investment, in 1992 MG created an elaborate hedging and marketing strategy involving the futures markets. Initially, this worked very well and began to show large paper profits. However, the company was long of 160 million barrels of oil in the futures market and, when oil prices collapsed towards the end of 1993, falling from $19 to $14 per barrel, massive margin payments became due almost daily and, by December of that year, MG had run out of the cash to pay them. The liquidation cost the company over $1 billion plus another $500 million to buy out existing contracts with the refinery. It was Germany's biggest post-war corporate disaster.

The bankruptcy of Orange County, a district of California, in 1994 was a combination of fraud on the part of the local government treasurer and some blatant churning by an American investment house. The County's entire investment pool was turned into a $1.7 billion deficit and the taxpayers will be paying for it for years to come. The county treasurer was elected to a seventh term of office earlier that year and had previously been outstandingly successful in building up the investment pool. However, he gambled everything on a bundle of derivatives in a deal that would only succeed if interest rates fell. They rose six times that year.

Market manipulation

Futures markets, from time to time, become the target of a certain amount of manipulation. Often these operations are very short lived, with one company taking advantage of a particular temporary situation and making a quick killing. Sometimes, however, they become more serious as attempts are made to squeeze or even corner a market.

An example of this was the July 1989 CBOT soyabeans contract, when one company held a long position of 22 million bushels (over seven times the speculative trading limit), accounting for 53% of the contract's total open interest. The company had also acquired ownership of over 85% of all cash market soyabeans available for delivery against the contract. The company claimed it was merely carrying out normal commercial hedging operations but the authorities felt otherwise and considered it to be trying to corner the market.

Even as the July contract approached its final days of expiration, the company showed no signs of liquidating its position and so the CBOT authorities decided to take action. Using its rarely employed emergency action, the CBOT ordered anyone with a position in excess of the three million bushel speculative limit (whether long or short) to liquidate those positions in an orderly manner, at the rate of 20% per day for the final five days to expiration.

Both the CBOT and CFTC are required by US law to prevent a potential market disruption and to protect the integrity of the market itself by ensuring orderly markets and position-holding procedures.

The present structure of futures markets in the world's leading financial centres makes it all but impossible – and prohibitively expensive – to acquire actual physical ownership of a high percentage of the entire supply of a commodity. This will not, of course, preclude a company from trying occasionally and it is important to have steps available to prevent that. The alternative would be contract defaults, as those on the opposite side of the market either refused – or were unable – to pay the manipulators' price.

Attempts at manipulation occur at regular intervals on the LME; during the first half of the 1990s all the metals traded had, at one time or another, been the target of such operations. The markets have been attacked by both merchants and speculators, the latter sometimes represented by managed funds. Nickel, in particular, will always be vulnerable to manipulation; a market of erratic supply and traditionally low stocks, it is often targeted at times of strikes and other supply disruptions.

In 1994, the LME copper price fell by a quarter in the space of just five weeks. This was followed by a supply squeeze when, in spite of lacklustre world economic conditions and high LME copper stocks, the price rose strongly. The LME committee issued two public warnings and eventually had to act by restricting the size of the daily backwardation. Among the losers was the China International Trust and Investment Corporation (CITIC), China's main overseas investment vehicle, which suffered losses of about $40 million owed to LME members who had extended credit to it.

The LME counteracts such activities by imposing daily borrowing limits when the cash premium has reached unacceptable levels. While effectively controlling the market, these position limits tend to bail out the victims, who do not really deserve such lenient action – after all, they entered into the contracts with their eyes open. It also breeds resentment from those members not involved. The LME has wide powers to fulfil its duty to maintain an orderly market: it can require a member to give any information needed, it can inspect members' trading records and it can get any details it wants from the clearing house. In addition, it has the power to suspend a member for up to 48 hours if suspected of disrupting a market.

One problem that needs to be addressed urgently is the manipulation of stocks in approved warehouses. This is, at times, quite flagrant; even when levels are quite high, it is noticeable that thousands of tonnes suddenly disappear off-warrant at the slightest sign of bullish news to help the price up, and are put back on again later when things have quietened down and profits been taken. The decision to report stock levels daily from April 1997 should help improve this situation.

A free market that cannot be dominated by any one operator is the goal of all market regulators but it is a fact of life that the manipulation of laws, without actually breaking them, can be a very lucrative pastime. It is the market regulators' duty to make those laws manipulation proof – not an easy task.

The more complicated the industry gets, the more sophisticated are the fraudsters; fraud gets more and more complex, and the regulators' jobs become more and more difficult. The requirement for all those handling client monies to be registered with the regulatory body has gone a long way towards stamping out the boiler-house tactics of the offshore bandits who cold-call likely targets in the UK and elsewhere, offering fantastic and totally impossible returns on investment in many a dodgy scheme – from non-existent gold mines to worthless shares being traded on obscure stock exchanges. The list is endless, with commodities featuring very highly. The 'churn 'em and burn 'em brigade', as these boiler-house operators are known, operate from empty offices in several different countries, and it is surprising how successful they can be sometimes in getting money from unwary and unsophisticated investors. It really is a case of *caveat emptor* as, in every situation, the money is lost for ever. Advice to help deal with these cold-callers is given below.

A recent survey of corporate treasurers in the USA found that one in five companies using derivatives ceased to do so during 1995. This was a direct result of the Barings collapse and indicative of the fear these markets generate in some quarters; there are still many in the markets who probably should not be. The survey also found that the remaining four-fifths actually increased their exposure, although there was a significant move away from the OTC markets and towards exchange-traded products. The reasons given for this trend were increased price transparency and less counterparty risk.

Perhaps the regulators still permit too much. Susceptible as they are to dire stories from vested interests of the imminent demise of the markets, they can feel intimidated into being less strict than the circumstances dictate. The vast rewards available on these markets cloud the judgement of all participants from the top echelons of a company to the very lowest; the prospect of a huge bonus has prompted many a manager to turn a blind eye to the excesses of his traders.

Cold-calling

The pernicious practice of cold-calling continues to plague the derivatives markets. These scams always emanate from a centre well away from the targeted clients: Canada and Holland have been popular places from which to target the United Kingdom. The practice has been largely outlawed but, as long as there are enough gullible punters to snare, there will be a continued danger of more attempts.

Usually peddling commodities or currencies, these salespeople can be very persuasive and at the slightest sign of interest are very tenacious, making extravagant promises of gigantic profits and/or amazing returns on investments. The best defence against being fleeced by these bandits is to ask if they are registered with the appropriate authority (e.g. the SFA) and to resist pressure to make any hurried decisions.

Other points to bear in mind are the following:

- Remember to get representations in writing.
- Be informed about market conditions.
- Ask how they got your name.
- Ask for references from a well-known bank.
- Get them to provide financial information and disclosure documents.

The most important point is the first one; it is an offence for anyone to give financial advice or to recommend a trade in a recognised exchange without being registered by the appropriate authority.

The importance of acquiring a comprehensive knowledge of any financial product before plunging in cannot be over-stressed. There is an army out there, unqualified and unregistered, just waiting to pounce upon unsophisticated investors and persuade them to part with their life savings in return for something that is too complicated to understand, often hidden within a jungle of jargon, and usually accompanied by wild promises of fantastic and unsustainable profits and/or returns. If in any doubt – stay out.

Conclusion

Although many of these past incidents can be blamed on one central cause – lack of credit control – lessons have been learned. After each one, credit has been tightened, internal controls have been reappraised and rules altered to prevent a recurrence. But credit itself is essential for the continued existence of a market; without it, it will die. In addition, there will always be rogue traders – increased controls will continue to make it harder for them but their techniques simply grow more sophisticated. Continual vigilance is the only way to prevent their activities. Personal gain is seldom the motive for such actions – it is more likely to be a desire for enhanced status, to be someone to whom the market defers before trading. Following the collapse of Barings Bank in 1995, the Futures Industry Association (FIA), a US-based industry watchdog, convinced a Global Task Force to co-ordinate the lessons learnt from it. In June of that year, it published its Financial Integrity Recommendations, comprising 60 recommendations for exchanges, clearing houses, intermediaries and clients. Sub-committees to oversee the implementation of these recommendations were formed, reporting in June 1996 by publishing an appendix to the original recommendations setting out their findings. If all the recommendations are implemented, the international futures and options markets will become far safer than they used to be.

Following any scandal as monumental as Barings or Sumitomo, the industry moves fast to learn the lessons and to implement any necessary changes to internal procedures and monitoring. Outside regulatory bodies hold inquiries into the scandals and make recommendations, but any overreaction to them or hasty decisions need to be avoided. After all, no investment house is going to sit back and allow it to happen to them. After Barings, City banks worked overtime checking their risk management and control systems, and the bank's collapse probably did more good to the trade than anything the regulators could do. Nevertheless, there are more rogue traders to be discovered in the future – there could be one out there even now, fleecing his employers. Constant vigilance is the one essential weapon to combat such activities.

CHAPTER

9

Regulation and compliance

It is the function of governments to look after the public interest and, in the context of regulating financial services, this may be defined as:

- protecting investors and customers of financial service providers (particularly retail or private investors) through, for example, business conduct, advertising and solicitation rules; the segregation of client money; mechanisms for customer redress; and the setting up of compensation funds;

- protecting counterparties, particularly through the imposition of capital requirements; and

- preventing destabilisation of the financial system, i.e. mitigation of systemic risk.

While these are the common objectives of national governments and regulatory authorities around the world, the ways in which they are achieved nationally and the priorities which are attached to those objectives vary considerably. In the case of cross-border business, for example, this can result in unnecessary regulatory duplication and conflict; a lack of regulatory transparency; statutory/protectionist clogs on market access; and legislative constraints on cross-border information flows and enforcement procedures.

Concerns over systemic risk have been exacerbated by the growing internationalisation of financial services, markets and products; the steady erosion of trade barriers; a continuing stream of new products and trading mechanisms; growth in product leverage; and changes in the size, complexity, functions and product-dealing distinctions of banks, institutions and brokerage houses. On the other hand, so far as derivatives are concerned, these concerns have been overstated because of misunderstandings over the amount at risk, i.e. it should be quantified in the context, not of the face value of a contract, but of the contractual income flows (probably no more than, say, 5% of the face value). Hence, although the amounts at stake are still significant, as the Chairman of the Basle Committee on Banking Supervision said in June 1994:

> Derivatives tend to reduce volatility under normal circumstances, enhance market efficiency, facilitate better pricing and provide low transaction costs. They also expand a range of hedging opportunities for market participants and thus lessen their dependence on any one particular market. In these ways, they dramatically improve the functioning of the financial system.

These needs to liberalise market access, harmonise regulation internationally and address systemic risk mean that regulators will have to adopt a more international and co-ordinated approach towards authorisation, monitoring, information sharing, auditing, investigation and enforcement procedures. Until recently, regulators had failed to mirror or, indeed, keep up with structural and other changes in institutions and markets by continuing to operate along product/geographical lines. This had put them out of step with the industry. Fortunately, this is increasingly becoming less the case. For example, common standards in rules are being agreed by international organisations such as the Basle Committee on Banking Supervision, the International Organisation of Securities Commissions (IOSCO) and the Group of 30 Study Groups and through memoranda of understanding and consolidated/lead regulation. Internationally, regulatory authorities are hoping to promote greater market transparency; better standards of best practice in accounting and disclosure; improvements in payment and settlement practices and systems; legal certainty in netting and customer/market dealings; greater rules transparency; and, perhaps most importantly, a more co-ordinated approach to systemic risk (e.g. through prompt management of market crises and 'fast-track' information disclosure).

While all of these moves are welcome advances in regulatory practice, it is equally true that this process of harmonisation could be as damaging to business as its absence. For example:

- A single solution or 'one size fits all' approach, which may simplify the job of regulators, can be deeply damaging to niche or individual markets, institutions, firms and financial centres (compare the need to preserve distinctive capital/regulatory treatment between banks and non-banks and between wholesale/retail financial services).

- There is a tendency, on the part of some international committees, to formulate cross-border principles behind closed doors, with little or no consultation with the industry.

- International agreement on minimum standards, by its nature, takes a long time to achieve and, for that very reason, it is often very difficult or even impossible to obtain a consensus for change.

- The negotiating process can exacerbate individual national interests and result in the politicisation of regulation.

The European Union

The establishment of the Single European Market has been achieved principally through the use of directives. These instruments require ratification by and are adopted and implemented through the domestic legislation of each member state. Proposals for financial service directives are the responsibility of Directorate-General XV of the European Commission, which is the legislative and executive arm of the European Union Markets. It is responsible for introducing legislation, overseeing the implementation of policy and initiating action against member states for infraction of European rules. The process of agreeing financial service directives is subject to the scrutiny of the European Parliament and, in particular, by either its Legal Affairs Committee or its Economic and Monetary Affairs Committee. The Council, which is made up of representatives of the governments of each member state, is responsible for taking the most important decisions, including the adoption of directives, usually by majority voting.

The principal directives and measures (to date) which impact on EU futures and options business are as follows:

- The removal of exchange controls (which may still be introduced by member states for periods not exceeding six months, but only in exceptional cases and then only with the authority of the Commission).

- The Banking Co-ordination Directives, which provide a minimum regulatory threshold for banks and facilitate the passporting of their activities across the Union.

- The Investment Services Directive, which gives non-banks rights both of establishment and to provide cross-border services anywhere in the Union and which establishes common authorisation criteria; notification and enforcement procedures; common principles for financial and business conduct rules; rights of access to member state exchanges; and a framework for information sharing and cross-border enforcement. The Directive does not cover marketing rules; clearing and settlement systems; criteria for the recognition of regulators, exchanges and clearing houses or regulation by exchanges and clearing houses of their own members. These matters fall within the individual discretion of member states. (NB: The Directive does not cover commodity futures and options or dealings in bullion.)

- The Capital Adequacy Directive (and related amending directives), which sets minimum capital requirements for brokers as well as the trading-book business of banks.

- The UCITS Directive provides a 'passport' for certain categories of collective investment schemes, principally security funds, and a minimum threshold for their regulation. While it provides for the use of futures and options for efficient portfolio management purposes, it does not extend to a passport to futures and options funds.

UK regulation*

In January 1985, the British Government published a White Paper (*Financial Service in the United Kingdom: A New Framework for Investor Protection*; Command 9432) which set out four essential objectives in seeking to establish a new regulatory framework, namely, efficiency, competitiveness, confidence and flexibility. In the event, while the Securities and Investments Board (SIB) and the regulatory bodies and agencies – particularly the Self Regulatory Organisations (SROs) – achieved much in a comparatively short space of time in setting up a regulatory structure to cover the range of sophisticated and complex financial services available in the United Kingdom, the industry felt that there had been a failure to achieve a proper balance in those original objectives. In particular, the prioritisation of investor protection had resulted in an unreasonable subordination of the other objectives of the White Paper and the cost, complexity and inappropriateness of the structure and some of the rules placed an intolerable and anti-competitive burden on UK financial service providers. It is significant that the pleas of the industry went unheard for a number of years, notwithstanding the promise of pragmatism held out by the establishment of a self-regulatory framework.

On a more positive note, there have been a number of welcome initiatives with a view to restoring that balance, e.g. the de-designation of rules to provide greater flexibility for SROs; the statutory duty recently imposed

---

* While this section is accurate at the time of printing, the government has announced radical changes to the restructuring of financial regulation through a significant enlargement in the scope and role of the Securities and Investments Board. These are likely to be introduced over the next two years.

upon regulatory authorities to assess the costs of compliance in developing and changing rules; reductions in the number of SROs; a more rational division of functions between SIB and the SROs; and the establishment of the Financial Law Panel to address areas of legal uncertainty. Nevertheless, there are continuing concerns that the statutory framework remains complex and unnecessarily fragmented, with too many authorities responsible for enforcement and too many tiers of regulation. As a result, the current regulatory framework is to be the subject of further overhaul. This will involve the assumption by the SIB of the Bank of England's supervisory role over banks followed by the merger of the SROs into the enlarged SIB. This would be a welcome simplification of the existing structure and should result in less duplication and, hopefully, real operational and infrastructure cost savings. On the other hand, there might be a propensity to adopt a framework of 'one glove fits all' regulation, which would be wholly inappropriate for a financial centre like London, which thrives on niche businesses and innovation in financial services. It could also result in greater bureaucracy which would make it difficult to achieve fast-track changes, which are absolutely vital if London is to retain its reputation for innovation. Clearly (and as always) it is a question of balance.

In the UK, the responsibility for regulating financial services is vested in HM Treasury by the Financial Services Act 1986 (FSA), the main provisions of which came into force on 29 April 1988. The performance of those responsibilities has been delegated to SIB. As the designated and semi-independent agency of HM Treasury, SIB has direct responsibility for the monitoring of SROs, exchanges and clearing houses (see below) as well as those professional associations whose members engage in investment business as part of their professional activities (e.g. lawyers, accountants).

The primary objectives of SIB are to achieve a high level of investor protection and to ensure firms meet minimum standards of honesty, competence and solvency. Its principal functions include:

- licensing (or recognising) and supervising UK SROs, stock and futures exchanges and clearing houses;
- exercising overall responsibility for international liaison on regulatory matters;
- enforcing the regulatory framework through the exercise of certain statutory powers, such as the issue of injunctions and the prosecution of offences;
- keeping and maintaining a register of all authorised persons and businesses.

Beneath SIB are the *Self* Regulatory Organisations (SROs). The SRO responsible for businesses engaged in the futures and options markets is called the Securities and Futures Authority (SFA). As its name implies, it is responsible also for authorising and regulating firms dealing in stocks and bonds. In other words, the UK has a single regulatory body for both derivative and cash-markets investment businesses. The SFA has approximately 1400 members, nearly two-thirds of whom carry on investment business in futures and options.

Next, there are the Recognised Investment Exchanges (RIEs). In order to be recognised by SIB, an RIE must have sufficient financial resources; ensure that business is conducted in an orderly manner and proper protection is afforded to investors; have adequate clearing arrangements; and be able to investigate complaints and monitor and enforce compliance with its rules.

In addition, there are the Recognised Clearing Houses (RCHs). The principal clearing house in the UK is the London Clearing House, which was first established in 1888 and is presently owned 75% by its members and 25% by the exchanges cleared by it. The members provide £150m of financial backing in cash, deposited in a special Member Default Fund. This is supplemented by an insurance policy, which provides an additional £100m worth of cover. The role of the London Clearing House is to register, clear and guarantee contracts traded on London's futures and options exchanges (the only exception being the London Securities and Derivatives Exchange (OMLX), which has its own internal clearing procedures). The advantages to users of the London markets are the provision of centralised clearing procedures across all multilateral settlement netting and the guaranteeing of contracts by a body which is broadly independent of the exchanges or their members and which has guarantee backing of £150m, provided by its bank owners.

The rules for futures and options business fall into four principal categories – the SIB Principles, which apply to all financial service activity and which provide a common core to individual SRO Rules; SRO rules, which govern the relationship between a firm and its customers; exchange rules, which regulate the floor trading of members; and clearing house rules, which address the clearing and settlement of exchange-traded contracts.

SRO rules

In broad terms, the SRO regulatory structure can be broken down into seven parts:

1 *Authorisation* (or a licence), which must be obtained from an SRO (in this case, usually the SFA) by any person or firm intending to carry on business in dealing, broking, giving advice on or managing derivatives. (NB It is the responsibility of SIB to recognise (or license) exchanges and clearing houses.) The overall objective is to ensure that all organisa-

tions, firms and individuals which engage in derivatives business are of good repute, competent and have sufficient resources to carry on that form of business. (NB This does not apply for non-UK/EU firms which may 'passport' their business with the UK based on their home state authorities.)

2 *Business conduct rules*, which require firms, for example:

- to enter into written agreements with private customers setting out the terms of business (including disclosing fees and commissions);
- to take account of the financial needs of their customers;
- to assess the suitability of transactions for customers;
- to take reasonable steps to ensure that the terms of the transaction are the best available in all the circumstances (otherwise known as giving 'best execution');
- to provide customers with a regular flow of information including risk disclosure statements, confirmation notes and periodic statements;
- to subordinate their own interests to those of their customers and to disclose any matter which may give rise to a conflict of interest.

Some of the more onerous rules can be disapplied in the case of non-private customers (e.g. business or professional customers) or customers who wish to be treated as non-private customers (e.g. because of their sophistication or experience).

3 *Advertising and marketing rules*, which are designed to prevent undesirable sales practices; control the marketing of illiquid investments; and ensure that advertisements and investment recommendations issued by firms are fair and not misleading (including the issue of risk warnings).

4 *Segregation rules*, which require authorised firms to hold and account for all customer monies in such a way as to protect the rights of customers, particularly in the event of the firm becoming insolvent. (NB Certain professional customers are permitted to opt out of segregation.)

5 *Financial rules*, which require members to maintain, at all times, minimum financial resources; to keep records and to submit regular financial statements and returns. These rules define classes of capital assets and risk exposures; set the ratios that those assets must bear to the exposures; and establish various weightings to cover, for example, market risk and counterparty risk.

6 *Enforcement rules*, which establish procedures for monitoring and investigating firms and provide for both regular and spot inspection of firms. In addition, there are disciplinary procedures which provide for a wide

range of sanctions in the case of breaches of the rules. These include public reprimand, fines, intervention in the running of the firm's business and/or expulsion from membership.

7 Lastly, there are *rights of redress*. While the regulations are intended to provide customers with a high level of protection, it is important that, where there are complaints and/or disputes, customers are provided with simple, economic and speedy means of seeking redress. These rights of redress, which are available to all customers of UK firms, whatever their nationality, comprise the following:

- Complaints procedures, whereby any person who has a complaint against a futures broker or dealer may, at any time (although usually after first bringing the matter to the firm's attention), refer his or her complaint for investigation to the relevant SRO (in this case, the SFA) or, in the event of a breach of an exchange's rules, to the relevant exchange.

- Conciliation procedures, whereby an SRO may be invited to act as an impartial mediator in a dispute involving one of its members.

- SRO arbitration, whereby any person may refer a dispute with a member of an SRO for determination by independent and experienced arbitrators appointed by the SRO, usually in consultation with the parties to the dispute.

- Exchange arbitration, whereby disputes between members may be resolved, but this procedure (and any related disciplinary proceedings) applies only to floor disputes and/or breaches in an exchange's rules.

- Compensation orders. The SFA disciplinary panel is empowered to award compensation during the course of a disciplinary hearing for the purpose of compensating an investor in respect of any readily determinable loss arising as a result of a breach of its rules.

In addition, customers suffering loss may seek redress by taking civil action in the UK courts (which includes a cost-effective small-claims procedure). In certain circumstances, SIB may exercise its statutory powers to seek injunctions, compensation, restitution and/or petition for the winding-up of a firm.

Any private customer who loses money as a result of an authorised futures firm going into liquidation may, provided the claim was incurred in the course of the firm carrying on authorised investment business, apply for compensation (up to a maximum of £48 000 per claim) to the Investors Compensation Scheme Limited. This is an independent company which has the responsibility of managing the Scheme and both the company and the Scheme are funded by a levy imposed on all authorised persons.

Exchange rules

Exchanges fulfil an essential regulatory role in ensuring that business is conducted in an orderly manner and that members are not only fit and proper, but also adequately resourced to support their trading activities. In general, exchange rules cover three basic areas: regulation of market participants, regulation of markets and regulation of the products traded on the markets. In addition, like the SROs, they undertake the investigation of complaints; monitor and enforce compliance with their rules; and provide arbitration facilities for the settlement of disputes. While exchange constitutions may vary considerably from exchange to exchange (e.g. some exchanges are privately owned, whereas others are owned by their members), their rules usually provide for governance by an elected Board of Directors drawn from market participants and the establishment of practitioner-based committees addressing such matters as membership, rules, disciplinary matters, etc.

Exchange rules can be divided into the following categories:

1 *Membership rules*, which are designed to ensure that traders can rely on the integrity and creditworthiness of their counterparties. These include 'fit and proper' criteria and require members to have adequate resources to support their trading activities. There may be several categories of membership, each of which carries different trading rights.

2 *Market regulation*, which is designed to ensure that, on a day-to-day basis, there is orderly conduct on the floor of the exchange. For example, there are rules on trading hours; rules preventing the dissemination of false information, the executing of false trades or market manipulation; and emergency rules covering, for example, the imposition of position limits, the suspension of trading and the increasing of margins.

   Pit officials can, for example, cancel trades in certain circumstances or refer them for further investigation. This will usually involve following what is known as an audit trail of order slips, trader cards, visual and telephone logs and transactions records.

3 *Contract rules*, which address such matters as specification and include, in the case of commodities, rules on the quality of goods, warehousing and points of delivery.

4 Rules providing for the *registration of transactions* and *publication of prices*.

5 Rules designed to safeguard the *performance of contracts* – whether cash-settled or by delivery of the underlying commodity or physical instrument – and which require the payment of deposits and margin. These are supported by clearing house rules (see below) which have the effect of ensuring that contracts traded on an exchange have the benefit of a guarantee.

Clearing house rules

Exchanges are dependent on their clearing houses to provide financially secure environments in which to trade their contracts. Clearing houses provide this environment through risk control measures, such as margining and the establishment of robust rules and procedures.

Clearing house rules can be divided into the following categories:

1 *Membership rules*, which include 'fit and proper' criteria and the imposition of capital requirements to ensure that members have sufficient financial resources to support their clearing activities. Typically, membership of a clearing house is a sub-set of the membership of exchanges cleared by it, although there may be more than one category of membership, each of which provides different clearing rights. Non-clearing members or users of an exchange will not usually be subject to the rules of the clearing house.

2 *Margining rules*, which are designed to ensure a clearing house has adequate margin available to meet losses it may incur as a consequence of closing or transferring the contracts of a defaulting clearing member. Typically, margin includes two components: variation and initial margin. The rules will normally specify the frequency at which margin is calculated and the criteria for the settlement of margin liabilities.

3 *Default rules* will normally provide for specific actions to be taken by the clearing house in order to manage the positions of a failed member. In some cases these may be supported by statutory insolvency provisions.

The Bank of England

Under Section 43 of the FSA, the Bank of England is given responsibility for maintaining a list of money market institutions that are exempt from the provisions of the FSA for their business in the Over-the-Counter (OTC) wholesale money markets. The conditions and arrangements drawn up by the Bank, as approved by HM Treasury, for administering this list are set out in its publication *The Regulation of the Wholesale Markets in Sterling, Foreign Exchange and Bullion* (otherwise known as the 'Grey Paper'). A major requirement of these arrangements is compliance with the London Code of Conduct, which sets out the standards expected by participants in the OTC cash and derivative wholesale markets. This function is quite separate from its role in monitoring and maintaining monetary and financial stability and the overall statutory duties and obligations imposed upon the Bank under the Banking Act 1987.

Summary

It is clear from the foregoing paragraphs that there is a comprehensive and effective framework of regulation that has been established for financial services. However, one of the lessons of some of the high-profile defaults and losses that have occurred in the last few years is that, no matter how complex a regulatory system, high standards in investor protection will not be achieved by relying solely on external regulation. As Alan Greenspan, Chairman of the US Federal Reserve, said:

> The amount of regulation in the broadest sense is escalating to match the proliferation of new products on the market, but there has to be self-regulation in this market, as Government regulation cannot do the job.

In other words, while self-regulation as the underlying philosophy behind the UK's regulatory framework may be – to use the words of the recent Treasury and Civil Service Committee Report – 'dying a natural death', governments and regulators should be grateful for the fact that it is still playing a major part in the front-line of investor protection.

- within the regulatory authorities, in the form of significant practitioner involvement in the evolution of rules and regulations;
- within firms, in the form of in-house compliance, through the maintenance of internal operational practices, procedures and controls, and through observance of ethical principles in business practice.

In addition to the increasing recognition given to the role of in-house controls and the move by regulators to risk-based supervision, there is a further argument that the well-publicised objective of the regulatory authorities, i.e. to protect investors, may have helped to lower the risk consciousness of customers and investors and encouraged the view that regulation is a form of guarantee against loss. It is this high expectation, placed on regulators, which has often resulted in accusations (often without justification) that they are not performing their role effectively. The fact is that there needs to be as much understanding about the limits on the capacity of regulation to deliver investor protection as there is about its benefits.

Aside from self-regulation and better understanding of the limits of regulation, perhaps the most effective means of furthering the cause of investor protection lies in customers and investors having a proper understanding of the risks of investment, i.e. the propensity for loss. It is interesting to note the response of Eddie George, Governor of the Bank of England, to criticism for not having bailed out Barings: 'the possibility of an individual bank failure is an essential discipline on the banking system'. By analogy, it can be argued that that very prospect of failure or loss is an equally essential discipline on investors and their attitude towards investment.

Moreover, while it is true that private investors, in general, enjoy (and should enjoy) higher standards of regulatory protection, the analogy is as true for them as it is for the wholesale end of the market.

Another of the most discussed aspects of regulation is its cost. Bearing in mind that, in the main, this is passed on as a business cost to customers and investors, it has a direct impact on the international competitiveness of firms, as well as on the amount of business being undertaken by customers and investors. To quote Eddie George again, referring to the trade-off between regulatory protection and regulatory cost:

> There is not much point in arrangements which provide absolute protection against risk in relation to financial transactions, if this means that the cost of those transactions puts them out of reach.

There is no doubt that government departments and regulatory authorities have a very difficult task in striking a proper balance between the needs of banks, institutions and firms regulated by them; the interests of the public and, in particular, customers and investors; the need to maintain international competitiveness; and concerns over regulatory cost. In essence, regulatory policy has to find the middle ground in a range of conflicting pressures:

1   The single-solution approach to regulation and in standards of investor protection can be inappropriate or even damaging to 'niche' business, products and financial service providers, as well as to particular types of investors and customers.

2   The social benefits of investor protection must be balanced against the commercial importance of allowing firms to be innovative and competitive and the need to maintain the economic benefits of free markets.

3   Rules and rule changes need to be assessed against a proper and effective cost/benefit analysis and regulators should be able to account publicly for their performance of that responsibility.

4   Regulatory or rules transparency is vital for effective regulation and is as important and beneficial to investors as market transparency (e.g. few rules well enforced are better than lots of rules inadequately enforced).

5   The judgemental and firm-focused approach of supervision is probably more appropriate for a sophisticated financial centre like London than the more mechanical 'box-ticking' approach adopted by some authorities.

6   Fast-track changes to regulation are of vital importance if investors are to be properly protected; financial centres are to be internationally competitive; and firms are to be able to develop new product lines

and new ways of business without being impeded by unnecessary or inappropriate regulation.

7   As a general rule, regulators should not seek to regulate matters of a purely commercial nature or assume the function of properly exercised commercial discretion without good cause.

8   Regulators must be as flexible and responsive to the needs of industry as to those of customers.

9   If regulators are to avoid being obliged to set impossibly high and unattainable standards in investor protection, they should take a more balanced role between cautioning investors about the limits of regulation and explaining its benefits.

10   Regulation is now an international and cross-border, cross-functional activity necessitating a more co-operative approach between regulators and a more comprehensive appraisal of the whole risk profile of individual firms.

The United States of America

In the USA, the regulatory framework for the trading of futures and options is governed by the Commodity Exchange Act 1936. In general, the Act requires all futures and options contracts to be traded on an exchange duly designated by the Commodity Futures Trading Commission (CFTC), unless otherwise exempted from the requirement by the CFTC (e.g. the 'swaps' exemption). The Act also prohibits a range of fraudulent activities involving futures and options trades including, for example, churning customer accounts and making false reports.

The CFTC is broadly responsible for regulating all futures and options business other than in relation to options on individual equities and equity indices, as well as certain other products of a financial nature, which come under the jurisdiction of the Securities Exchange Commission (SEC). In particular, the CFTC is responsible for overseeing the registration of brokerage firms and market professionals; imposing minimum capital regulatory standards; preventing trading malpractice, including price manipulation, excessive speculation, the dissemination of false market information and fraudulent activity as regards the solicitation of customer accounts or the execution of trades; and protecting customer funds. The CFTC is also responsible for the general oversight of US futures and options exchanges and imposes a number of specific regulatory requirements on them. However, exchanges are also treated as SROs in their own right.

The National Futures Association (NFA) is an SRO registered with the CFTC and to which has been delegated the task of registering brokerage houses; setting financial requirements for its members; establishing and enforcing rules and standards for customer protection; and providing arbitration facilities in relation to futures and options disputes.

While there are certain fundamental differences in the basis of regulation between the UK and the USA, the overall US regulatory structure is, in broad terms, very similar to that prevailing in the UK. Some of the more specific differences include the following:

- In the USA, the responsibility for regulating securities and futures business is vested in two separate regulatory authorities, i.e. the CFTC and the SEC, whereas in the UK the regulatory function has been merged into a single regulatory authority, the SFA.

- US exchanges have to obtain specific CFTC approval before listing new contracts and must be able to demonstrate that a new contract will satisfy an economic purpose, whereas in the UK exchanges may list new contracts as they see fit, although this will usually involve prior consultation with SIB.

- In the USA, all futures and options should be traded on an exchange or be exempted by the CFTC. In the UK, there is no such constraint.

- In the USA, a Joint Audit Committee has been established to prevent unnecessary duplication in regulatory auditing procedures, with the result that oversight of a specific brokerage house becomes the responsibility of a Designated Self-Regulatory Organisation (DSRO), which may be the NFA or an exchange. In the UK, there is no such committee, although SROs and exchanges do co-ordinate audit visits or conduct them jointly.

- In the USA, ethics training is compulsory, whereas in the UK it is voluntary.

- There are differences in specific regulatory requirements between the two jurisdictions (e.g. unlike in the UK, segregation is compulsory in the USA with no opt-out, and US brokerage houses are allowed to guarantee the financial integrity of their introducing brokers).

- In the USA, there are much tighter constraints on the giving of credit to customers, whereas in the UK the regulatory authorities adopt a more flexible approach where firms' credit management procedures satisfy regulatory requirements.

- In the USA, market dealings are subject to additional controls such as position limits by CFTC and by the exchanges and there is a less clear distinction between wholesale and retail business (eg. there are more rules exemptions available for wholesale business in the UK than in the USA).

- While there are definite similarities in the financial regulation of firms in the USA and the UK, the UK system is risk based, whereas in the USA, there is greater focus on segregated funds.

Notwithstanding the foregoing differences, there is sufficient commonality in the regulatory framework for futures and options business between the USA and the UK to justify cross-border market access on the basis of mutual recognition in standards of investor protection. While there are arguments over whether there is reciprocity in access between the two jurisdictions, it is hoped that the globalisation of futures and options business, and international moves to liberalise trade in financial services, will generate an increasing degree of reciprocity, and the eventual establishment of full cross-licensing of firms, between the UK and the USA.

10

Training and education

The effectiveness of self-regulation and the maintenance of high standards in investor protection are, in large part, dependent upon the individual competence, knowledge and ethical standards of those engaged in the futures and options industry. The requirements of law and the regulations of the Securities and Futures Authority (SFA) set minimum acceptable standards, particularly in the areas of best market practice and business conduct.

While trading forward in order to manage price risk has been an integral part of world trade for centuries, it is only in the last decade that futures trading has become a financial service industry in its own right, ranking alongside banking, insurance and securities. It is not altogether surprising therefore that the educational and examination structure applicable to those engaged in such business is not as mature as in other financial service sectors. Even so, considerable advances have been made with the development of the following:

- minimum regulatory education requirements centred on the SFA's Registrered Representative examinations and training of floor traders by exchanges;
- the Securities Institute's Diploma and related courses;
- the number of basic, intermediate and advanced courses and seminars provided by independent professional trainers.

In addition to entry training and examinations, the SFA requires firms to 'undertake and provide training to ensure adequate competent standards in accordance with the nature of the business done by the firm and the individual'. This means that firms are required to put in place procedures to ensure that all their staff are aware of relevant regulatory requirements and are kept up to date with developments in the markets. The objective is to ensure that not only are they competent but they continue to remain competent by keeping abreast of knowledge relevant to their work. Firms are given broad flexibility to ensure that the range, type and extent of continuation training is relevant to indiviudal employees, but firms are subject to the monitoring of SFA audit teams who will pay particular attention to the training of Registered Representatives involved in advising private clients.

Registered Representative examination

The SFA is the regulatory authority responsible for authorising and regulating firms which carry on investment business in futures and options. In addition to its overall function of ensuring that such firms are and continue to be 'fit and proper' for the purpose of carrying on their business, it makes a similar appraisal of individuals to ensure that they can reasonably be expected to perform their duties efficiently, honestly and fairly. In making this appraisal, SFA will look at a range of matters including reputation, character, experience and education qualifications. Hence, all essential employees of SFA member firms are required to register indiviually with SFA. This applies to senior individuals in a position of responsibility (e.g. senior executive officers, directors, partners and managers), those who give investment advice (e.g. account executives, salespeople, etc.); those who commit their firms in dealings with other professionals (e.g. traders and 'yellow jackets') and other staff in positions of authority (e.g. compliance officers and financial officers).

The registration requirement is coupled with linked training and eduction programmes, the purpose of which is to provide a framework by which customers, firms and regulators may be assured that all persons engaged in trading or advising on futures and options meet minimum standards of competence and knowledge. This is achieved by requiring individuals to sit the relevant Registered Person examination(s), which take a variety of forms and are dependent upon the financial service activity undertaken by the individuals in question.

Courses for SFA's Futures and Options Representatives examinations are provided by a number of independent colleges and training establishments (details of which may be obtained from the Futures and Options

Association or the Securities Institute). Candidates are tested on their knowledge of relevant legislation and SFA's Conduct of Business and other rules as well as on markets, trading practices and procedures, margining and clearing.

Depending upon how the individual wishes to tailor the examination, its length may vary between three and five hours and may consist of between 150 and 250 multiple-choice questions. The basic examination covers regulatory matters and deals with markets and derivative instruments. Further modules may be taken separately to enhance the basic qualification and increase its scope. Sittings are held at least twice weekly in London (according to demand) and at regular intervals at regional centres in the UK and in Dublin. Training is available via both full-time courses and distance learning.

Once candidates have passed the Futures and Options Representative examination, they qualify and are registered as Futures and Options Registered Representatives and become eligible to give investment advice in futures and options. Alternatively, a candidate may elect to sit the SFA's General Registered Representative examination, which will entitle the successful candidate to advise on a broader range of financial instruments, including equities and interest rate instruments.

SFA recognises a number of overseas equivalent examinations, and holders of these qualifications may be granted full or partial exemption (depending on their experience and the level of the qualification) from the Futures and Options Registered Representative examination. Equally, a number of overseas jurisdictions which have their own training and education requirements recognise the SFA Registered Representative qualification, with the result that individuals wishing to work in those jurisdictions may also be granted full or partial exemption from domestic financial service qualification examinations. Hence, in the USA, an SFA qualified Registered Representative would be exempted from sitting the full Series 3 Examination, providing they meet the US ethics training requirement and sit the regulation module of the Series 3 Examination (otherwise known as the Series 32 Examination). The Futures and Options Association provides all the necessary training and can arrange for SFA Registered Representatives to sit the Series 32 Examination.

While delivery of the Registered Representative examination is the responsibility of the Securities Institute, SFA retains responsibility for overall policy, syllabus and examination questions. In view of the periodic revising of SFA's registered and related examinations (for the purpose of ensuring that they are in line with the current working environment), anyone interested in sitting the examinations should contact the Securities Institute.

Exchange training programmes for floor traders

The floor trader training programmes of each of London's futures and options exchanges are designed to provide floor traders with the requisite knowledge and skills to trade their contracts. While there are no specific educational requirements for trainees, it is clearly an advantage to have a degree or a number of A-levels. It should always be borne in mind that being a floor trader is a high-pressure job – always exciting, sometimes stressful – and, while trading times will vary from exchange to exchange, it usually involves working long hours.

The *London International Financial Futures and Options Exchange* (LIFFE) training programme comprises a preliminary induction course and one month's experience on the floor before any candidate becomes eligible to register for the Floor Traders Course. The induction course comprises a basic introduction to LIFFE, its structure and systems. The Floor Traders Course is taken in two stages addressing, successively, theory and practice. The theory comprises six computer-based training modules and exams covering futures contracts, financial aspects of futures trading, off-line management, rules and procedures and the language of LIFFE futures and options. Once a candidate passes the theory, he or she may move on to the practical exam which comprises three training sessions on the LIFFE floor (after the floor has closed) and an exam on the fourth night, followed by a panel interview. Only then may a trader apply for a 'blue button' and trade on the floor, albeit under supervision. After a period of three months, or in some cases less, the trader is again interviewed and assessed as to his or her ability to trade unsupervised.

The Commodities Products Department of LIFFE provides an open-learning course in hard-copy form in five separate modules covering a general introduction to the LIFFE's commodities products, market rules and regulations, how to make a bid and offer, trading and confirmation systems, administrative paperwork and disciplinary procedures. Once the trainee has completed the learning programme and passed an examination, he or she will then become a 'red badge', which allows a trainee to trade under supervision until such time as it is considered that he or she has obtained a suitable level of competence.

LIFFE supplements in Floor Traders examinable courses by running a number of detailed but non-examinable seminars on futures and options trading and back-office procedures. The course on back-office procedures, which has been enlarged to include commodity futures and options, is followed by an optional examination. In addition, there is a mandatory Automated Trading System (APT) course for all those who have signed to use LIFFE's new system.

The *International Petroleum Exchange* (IPE) provides an intensive five-stage Registered Floor Trader Qualification programme. All new entrants to the IPE are required to register with the Exchange Training Manager who, in conjunction with the Floor Committee and Exchange Floor Manager, supervises their training and qualification schedule. The programme includes a preliminary two-day induction course, a self-study Modular Traders Course, three examinations, a three-month probationary trading period, a practical exam and a Traders Review Panel.

Additionally, the IPE offers its members and users a wide range of training courses which specialise in contract briefings, futures trading traded options seminars (Introductory, Intermediate and Advanced) and risk management workshops.

The *London Metal Exchange* (LME) training programme is dependent upon a mix of practical hands-on training, a period of 'clerkship' and a comprehensive oral test and interview. This is followed by a period of probation comprising not less than six months' supervised working on the trading floor. Following a further interview of the probationer, he or she may then become an authorised dealer.

The *OMLX* (London Securities and Derivatives Exchange) provides a training course for prospective members covering all aspects of the Exchange's functioning. This includes clearing, administration and trading. Members requiring electronic access must undergo training in the use of OMLX's Click trading system before they can be accredited as Authorised Traders.

The *London Clearing House*, together with the exchanges, runs and supports an education programme which provides delegates with knowledge and practical guidance to help maintain high standards of settlement and clearing. Courses are attended by staff (from LCH, member firms and the exchanges) who are involved with the administration of back-office/settlement procedures. In addition, LCH offers its own staff a wide range of training modules, covering everything from specialised in-house systems training to external supervisory and general management programmes.

Additional courses and training

The *Securities Institute* is the professional body for individual practitioners from a broad range of financial services businesses. Whilst the majority of its Members, Associates and Student Members are drawn from the Stock Exchange area, many of them are practitioners in other fields such as fund and asset management, corporate finance, investment administration and financial futures and options.

The Institute's role is to promote high standards of integrity and, through its work in the area of training and qualifications, to set and maintain high standards of professional competence. It has 19 branches in the UK and offshore, and publishes a monthly professional journal.

The Institute's educational programme can be summarised as comprising the following:

- A Foundation Programme, which includes delivery of the SFA Futures and Options Registered Reprensentative examination and a series of voluntary training and testing modules under the general title of 'Investment Administration Qualifications'.

- Continuation training, which is designed to provide an opportunity for practitioners to keep up to date with the latest regulatory and market developments.

- Professional education, which is centred on the Institute's Diploma. The Diploma is awarded when three from a range of nine specialised exams have been passed.

The Diploma is the route to membership of the Institute for most applicants, although the qualifications of other professional bodies and academic institutions may be recognised as satisfying, in part, the Institute's educational criteria. Student Members are offered seminars and publications to support their studies.

The *Futures and Options Association* (FOA) is a London-based trade association for firms, institutions and exchanges involved in futures and options business. One of its main objectives is to promote better knowledge and understanding of derivatives, and this is achieved through the provision of technical workshops, courses and briefings which assist participants in meeting regulatory continuation training requirements, while also raising levels of competence generally within the industry.

Further information can be obtained from the Futures and Options Association, whose address can be found in Appendix B.

11

The taxation of futures and options

As is all too often the case with many areas of taxation, the taxation treatment of futures and options both in the UK and overseas is far from clear-cut. This is not wholly surprising considering the comparatively recent introduction of these instruments and their complexity. The essential problem regarding the taxation of derivative products is that taxation legislation is constantly and unavoidably lagging behind the developments of the instruments in the market-place.

This constant state of 'catch-up' has implications not only for the taxation authorities in various countries, but obviously also for the users of the instruments, whether these users are financial traders, corporate bodies or individuals. It is of key importance to be aware of the likely tax consequences of using futures and options products for hedging or speculation before using such products, yet these consequences vary widely between users and between countries. Further, the timing of the tax charge can be of equal significance.

This chapter therefore attempts to identify and summarise the key principles of taxation legislation in the UK, Europe and the USA.

United Kingdom

The taxation treatment of futures and options contracts in the UK has historically revolved around the familiar tests of whether the profit from such products represents trading income or capital gains. However, two recent major changes to UK legislation have specifically addressed the taxation treatment of a number of futures and options instruments. As these new rules impact on different users to differing extents, the taxation treatment of futures and options in the UK is best discussed in terms of market users.

Banks and financial institutions

This grouping includes all users carrying out a bona fide trade in financial instruments, the main examples of which are banks and derivative traders. This grouping has, in general, been unaffected by the recent changes in tax legislation.

Clearly, banks and financial institutions are trading futures and options, and accordingly the Inland Revenue will generally assume that any transactions in futures and options should be treated as revenue and so deemed to fall on trading account. As such, any profits or losses will be subject to tax under Schedule D Case I, which is the usual method for assessing trading income.

The tax treatment of financial traders generally follows the accounting treatment. The Inland Revenue has, in the past, indicated that the strict method for computing taxable profits or losses is by taking into account realised transactions only. However, the Inland Revenue is now generally willing to accept accounts prepared on both an accruals and mark-to-market basis. Some uncertainty may still exist regarding the precise method of mark-to-market policy used by a financial trader. Various reserves, for example, are made by trading companies in the course of marking positions-to-market and these reserves are increasingly being questioned by the Inspectors of Taxes.

Corporate users

The taxation treatment of futures and options for corporate users has been most heavily affected by the recent changes in taxation legislation. Previously, it would have been possible to discuss all types of futures and options contracts in terms of whether the contracts were of a trading or capital nature. However, it is now, perhaps, more beneficial to discuss the taxation treatment of specific types of contracts.

COMMODITY FUTURES AND OPTIONS

In the UK, there is only limited specific legislation in respect of the taxation treatment of traded commodity futures and options. As a result, most treatment follows general tax legislation and Inland Revenue accepted practice in respect of such transactions.

As such, transactions in commodity futures and options by companies are segregated between capital and revenue. The application of this approach means that if a transaction is ancillary to a trading transaction on a current account, the related profit or loss is a trading profit or loss. This profit or loss would therefore be included within Schedule D Case I. This has the advantage that any ancillary costs associated with the purchase of such an options or futures contract will be fully deductible for tax purposes.

Where the transaction is a non-trading transaction, the profit or loss is capital in nature. The gains or losses on such capital transactions are taxed on a realisations basis.

It may be the case that the futures or options transaction is not clearly ancillary to another transaction. In this instance it may be possible to prove that the transaction was a trading transaction in its own right. In order to establish whether a trading transaction exists in this situation the Inland Revenue will take the 'Badges of Trade' into consideration. These are, *inter alia*, the number of transactions, intention, experience of the markets, the making of the actual trading decisions, the amount of time devoted and the method of financing.

INTEREST RATE AND CURRENCY FUTURES AND OPTIONS

Interest rate and currency futures and options are the first type of such instruments to have been subject to the recently introduced legislation. In the past, these types of financial instruments had followed the general tests and treatment outlined above for commodity futures and options. The overall effect of the changes has therefore been to include more contracts within the charge to tax and simultaneously reduce the incidence of chargeable gains.

Definitions introduced with the new legislation determine exactly which futures and options are included in the new legislation. A detailed definition of the various terms is outside the scope of this chapter, but most types of interest rate futures and options and currency futures and options of the types commonly used to hedge interest rate and currency exposure are included.

For contracts included under the new rules, where a company's accounting treatment of qualifying financial instruments follows generally accepted accounting practices, the recognition of profits or losses for tax purposes will follow the accounts.

Profits and losses are then characterised according to whether they relate to the trade, and accordingly are classified as trading income or non-trading income. This distinction is a different test to the trading/capital test applied under the previous rules. For example, some items that would previously have been classed as capital may now be treated as trading profits or losses.

Trading income is taxed under Schedule D Case I. The key distinction under the new rules is that the non-trading income is taxed under Schedule D Case III. As such, these non-trading profits are taxed on a revenue basis and are not subject to chargeable gains. Furthermore, trading losses may be offset against other revenue included in either Case I (for trading losses) or Case III (for non-trading losses).

The treatment of non-trading losses under the new rules is more favourable than the position for traded commodity futures and options. If, once the losses have been offset against other revenue, a net Schedule D Case III loss exists, this loss may be offset against all other income as a charge on income. This contrasts with the position for capital losses: these may only be offset against capital gains, which in some cases proves restrictive.

DEBT INSTRUMENTS FUTURES AND OPTIONS

Derivatives over debt instruments are the most recent category of futures and options to have been specifically included in taxation legislation. This legislation came into effect as recently as 1 April 1996, and so it is perhaps not yet possible to discuss with a great deal of certainty the full impact of these changes. In addition, it should be noted that a number of transitional provisions are included in these new rules which are beyond the scope of this chapter.

Essentially, as a result of the recent legislation, futures and options over debt instruments will be treated in line with the taxation treatment of the underlying debt. Most debts are included within the new rules and are referred to as 'loan relationships'. These loan relationships have again been specifically defined within the legislation and include gilts held by companies, corporate bonds, permanent interest-bearing shares, and other corporate debt.

All profits and losses made on these debts will be treated as revenue profits or losses. This in reality means that capital profits and losses that were previously dealt with by calculating chargeable gains on a realisation basis are now taxed as revenue, generally on an accruals or mark-to-market basis. Similarly, profits or losses relating to futures and options over these debts will be treated in a consistent manner. As for interest rate and currency futures and options, this results in profits and losses being taxed under Schedule D Case I (for trading revenue) or Schedule D Case III (for non-trading revenue). Again, losses may be offset against other income included within the appropriate Case. A net Schedule D Case III loss may be offset against all other income as a charge on income.

The introduction of the new government and corporate debt taxation in effect treats futures and options over these debts in similar manner to interest rate and currency futures and options.

EQUITY FUTURES AND OPTIONS

As equity futures and options are dealt with mainly by financial institutions, there is little taxation legislation addressing their taxation in the hands of other corporate bodies. Once again however, the general trading/capital distinction can be drawn upon to offer guidance on the taxation principles governing the profits and losses arising from their use.

As with commodity futures and options, derivatives relating to equities are in many cases taxed in line with the taxation of an associated underlying asset. Again, in the case of a futures or options transaction that is not clearly ancillary to another transaction, the transaction could be argued to be trading subject to satisfying the 'Badges of Trade' test.

Individuals

Individuals entering into options or futures contracts will see the taxation treatment of gains or losses from such contracts following one of two directions. Gains could be taxed either as income on a trading basis, or alternatively as capital gains. In relation to capital gains there is the advantage of an annual exemption (£6300 in 1996/7) for each individual. Most individuals are broadly unaffected by the recent introduction of new rules governing the taxation of debt, interest rate and currency futures and options.

Four different types of situation could be envisaged, as follows.

TRADERS

Individuals carrying on a bona fide trade in financial futures or options will be taxed under Schedule D Case I. Profits will be treated as earned income and taxed on a current-year basis. New current-year rules for assessing income under this Schedule come into effect in the fiscal year 1996/7. Previously, earned income was assessed on a prior-year basis, although a number of temporary rules have been implemented in the transitional period. The existence of a trade continues to be established by reference to the presence of the 'Badges of Trade' already referred to above.

SPECULATORS

Where an individual speculates in financial futures or options listed on a recognised exchange, then capital gains tax rules apply. It must be remembered, however, that where speculation becomes very frequent and involves a considerable input of time on the part of the individual, then the Inland Revenue may seek to tax the activity as a trade.

INCOME ENHANCEMENT

A UK resident individual with, say, US dollars on deposit might seek to enhance the income on that account by selling out-of-the-money currency options. If the option remains until maturity without any exercise notice being issued, then the premium income will be taxed as a capital gain. Again, though, if there is considerable frequency of such activity, this may lead to trading treatment.

HEDGING INVESTMENTS

Individuals with commodities, securities and foreign currency deposits in their investment portfolio might use futures, equity options and currency options to hedge the value of that portfolio. Provided there is a specific link to underlying investments and there is a correlation to the underlying risk, capital gains tax should apply to contracts on recognised exchanges.

Specialist users

PENSION FUNDS

Approved pension funds receive specific taxation treatment so that income or capital gains derived from investments are exempt from both income and capital gains taxes. With the development of financial futures and traded options, it became unclear as to whether the use of such products by approved funds and schemes fell within the exemption.

This position has now been clarified, with both financial futures and traded options being expressly included in the definition of investments, hence granting tax-exempt status for pension funds on profits from non-trading transactions.

UNIT TRUSTS AND INVESTMENT TRUSTS

Authorised unit trusts are exempt from capital gains tax. Where a futures or options contract is taken out specifically to hedge underlying assets, this should lead to capital gains tax treatment, i.e. exemption. Profits of authorised unit trusts which are derived from dealing in futures and options are also exempt from tax. However, a careful approach to the situation is required, notwithstanding the above, because income of a non-dealing nature, for example interest on deposits placed with futures and options brokers, will remain taxable.

Investment trusts are also exempt from capital gains tax. As for authorised unit trusts, the gain or loss on futures or options contracts taken out to hedge underlying assets will be treated as capital. This is particularly critical for an investment trust as any significant profit level of trading income may result in the company breaching the requirements for the special tax status. Investment trusts have also been affected by the new interest, currency and debt instruments futures and options legislation. For example, although non-trading interest rate and currency contracts are treated as taxable under Schedule D Case III, these non-trading profits will be treated as income from shares or securities for the purposes of the special tax status requirements. This is a particularly difficult area of taxation and specialist advice should be taken.

Europe

As tax treatment varies on a country-by-country basis, it is impossible to generalise about the taxation treatment of futures and options throughout Europe. Accordingly, a sample of countries has been selected for detailed discussion.

Belgium

There are no specific tax rules in Belgium with respect to futures or options. Taxable income should be determined according to the accounting rules unless the tax law provides for specific exception. Consequently, the way a futures or options transaction is recorded in the accounts will determine the tax regime.

The distinction between hedging and speculative transactions will prevail for tax purposes. However, the application of the general principles leaves, to a certain extent, the possibility of anticipating or deferring certain gains or losses and costs generated by or associated with these instruments. Any tax planning opportunities will therefore mainly concentrate on the timing of the profit or loss recognition. These opportunities may be significant in relation to the utilisation of tax loss carry-forwards, non-refundable tax credits or anticipated changes in tax rates.

Finally, it is worth mentioning that the Belgian tax law has introduced substance-over-form legislation. This represents anti-abuse legislation whereby the tax authorities are not bound by the legal qualification of an act. The application of this legislation means that if a finance operation is structured in such a way that it may receive two legal qualifications, the tax authorities may change the legal qualification selected by the taxpayer so that higher taxes will be due, unless the taxpayer can demonstrate that this qualification meets legitimate financial or economic needs.

France

The tax treatment of derivatives trading by companies resident in France is mainly governed by recent legislation, as clarified by Administrative Comments dated 20 April 1988.

Contracts on non-hedging transactions on all futures, forwards and options that are quoted or traded 'on a market or by reference to a market' must be marked-to-market at the year end, and the resulting gain or loss included in current taxable income.

On contracts traded outside a market, the unrealised gains can be deferred until after the contract is settled.

Where contracts are traded specifically as a hedge against risks from transactions in the two subsequent years, and disclosure is made to the tax administration, tax on unrealised gains may be deferred until the contracts are settled.

Where contracts are traded specifically as a hedge against exchange risks on future operations, and disclosure is made to the tax administration, tax on unrealised gains may be deferred until the hedge operation is settled.

Positions may be offset with the following limitation: where one position has a gain which has not been taxed, the fraction of the loss, realised and/or unrealised, on the offsetting position corresponding to the untaxed gain is not deductible. In such a case, subject to the appropriate disclosure, the deduction is held off until the gain is taxed.

Special rules apply to swap transactions entered into by French credit institutions.

Germany

The tax treatment of futures and options for *business investors* follows the accounting treatment. Profits are taxed as income at standard rates for individual or corporate income tax and municipal trade tax on income. Corporations' and individuals' holdings of options are subject to capital taxes.

For *private investors*, premiums received by the writer are taxed as income at standard rates. Premiums paid for closing transactions are deductible expenses. It is, however, not possible to offset losses suffered in the underlying assets or liabilities against the premium.

Following recent court decisions, those gains and losses that arise on the disposal of an option are treated as net capital gains. Gains must be short-term (under six months), and worth more than DM 999 per year, before they will be subject to tax.

The current position on gains from futures is that they are tax free to private investors because they are seen to be gambling profits. This follows an official statement of the Federal Ministry of Finance dated 10 November 1994 on the taxation of Deutsch Terminbörse (DTB) trades for private investors.

There is no longer a stock exchange turnover tax or stamp duty. Options and futures are not subject to value added tax.

Luxembourg

In general, the tax treatment of futures and options transactions in Luxembourg follows the accounting treatment. Consequently, all losses on futures and options transactions are deductible from income (whether realised or otherwise) but only those gains that have been realised will be subject to tax. Unrealised gains are not taxed until the contract is settled. This is obviously an advantageous taxation regime in terms of the favourable timing difference this provides.

Some flexibility is also provided by the taxation regime, in that both hedging profits and losses deferred in the accounts may be deferred for tax purposes.

A further benefit can be obtained for tax purposes if futures and options are invested in Luxembourg through a collective investment fund. Luxembourg is a recognised centre for the European and worldwide investment fund industry, and the first specifically authorised funds invested in options in 1978. These funds provide the usual benefits associated with any mutual investment, such as access to futures and options (to an investor who might not on a stand-alone basis have the capital required for a direct investment) and a diversification of risk. In addition, investment funds in Luxembourg are exempt from tax on all income and gains but subject to an annual tax of 0.06% or 0.03% on net asset value.

The Netherlands

The Netherlands does not have a general capital gains tax for individuals. A capital gain can be taxed only in very specific situations, for example when a profit is realised as a consequence of insider trading. Except in these specific situations and for those individuals who are trading, there is no income tax or capital gains tax impact on individuals with gains and losses resulting from transactions in futures and options. However, derivatives are brought into net equity for the calculation of net equity tax. They are taxed on the 1 January value at 0.8%.

In the case of professional traders, prudent business principles are applied. Until fiscal year 1992 the tax authorities accepted a system whereby long positions were valued at the lower of cost and market value, and short positions at the higher of cost and market value. In this way realised gains and losses were treated as normal trading income and expenditure; whereas unrealised profits could be deferred and unrealised losses included. In practice, however, this led to a reduction in the value of the securities to a rather unrealistic level. The question is, therefore, whether these positions should be matched for valuation principles.

Presently no clear case law is available on the matching issue. Meanwhile the Dutch tax authorities have issued a ruling in respect of market makers dealing on the European Options Exchange in Amsterdam. According to the ruling, securities positions relating to a certain fund will have to be categorised in order of their lifetimes. For each category the matching principle will be applied. Subsequently, for each category the total cost price and market value will have to be determined. A predominant long position will then be valued at the lower of cost and market value, whilst short positions will be valued at the higher of cost and market value.

This valuation system only seems to apply for options and security positions. For other financial instruments, the old valuation system can still be applied. According to the present jurisprudence it can be gathered that only when a 100% correlation exists between the underlying asset and the financial instrument, will a perfect hedge be deemed present. Only in these 100% matched situations will the matching principle have to be applied. In other situations there is a defence for the positions to be separately valued.

Switzerland

In Switzerland the tax treatment of income is generally determined by the accounting treatment used. Thus the method of taxation used for futures and options follows the accounting treatment.

Gains made by individuals on derivatives trading are exempt from federal tax as long as the trading activity does not qualify as a professional business. Those gains which can be defined as private capital gains are also exempt from tax in all but one of the 26 Cantons. Net capital gains are, however, taxed in the remaining Canton.

Trading in futures and options will not incur duty (except in cases of physical delivery of securities) and options held by individuals are subject to regular wealth tax. No withholding tax is charged on SOFFEX.

However, new kinds of derivative instruments, which combine the characteristics of an option and a money market investment or a bond, have appeared in the market. These instruments (GROI, GRIPS, etc.) usually guarantee the initial investment to the investor at maturity while the yield depends on the variation in price of a share, an index, etc. Such instruments are considered by the tax authorities as either bonds or money market deposits. Therefore, in general any payment in excess of the initial investment is taxable income and subject to withholding tax if issued by a Swiss issuer. In addition to this, a stamp tax of 0.6 per million for each full or partial year of the maximum term is due on the nominal value and is levied on the issuance.

United States of America

Whether profits and losses resulting from options other than Section 1256 contracts not utilised as a hedge (these contracts are described below) are treated as capital or ordinary income depends on the property underlying the option. If capital asset treatment applies and the option is held for more than one year, long-term capital gains or losses will be recognised when the option lapses or is disposed of. Any premium paid will be treated as a non-deductible capital expenditure. Any premium received is not included in income at the time of receipt but will be recognised at the time of exercise, expiration or disposal.

Section 1256 contracts are regulated futures contracts, foreign currency contracts, non-equity options and dealer equity options trading on qualifying exchanges, and may be taxed under the year-end mark-to-market rules. Generally, adjustments to basis are made when the position is closed. Unrealised gains and losses are marked-to-market at year end and treated as 60% long term and 40% short term. Certain forward foreign currency contracts traded in the inter-bank market result in ordinary income or loss.

In certain cases Section 1256 contracts are used for hedging purposes. Generally the mark-to-market and 60/40 rules will not apply where the hedge is entered into in the normal course of the taxpayer's trade or business to reduce the risk of price change, currency fluctuation or interest change. Gain or loss is ordinary if the transaction is identified under hedging regulations. The timing of gain or loss must reasonably match the item being hedged under accounting method regulation.

Dealers in securities are required to carry their securities inventory at fair market value. In the absence of certain identifications, any non-inventory securities owned by a dealer are marked-to-market at year end. For corporations, there is currently no difference in tax rates between capital and ordinary income but capital losses may only be deducted to the extent that they offset capital gains.

Individual taxpayers may receive a benefit for net long-term capital gains versus net short-term capital gains and ordinary income.

Conclusion

The taxation of financial futures and options in Europe and the USA is an evolving area of legislation. The speed of development of financial markets means that markets will be ahead of existing tax law for most countries. There are a number of common themes that can be traced between users and countries, but in general a discussion of the differing tax regimes both within and between countries only serves to re-emphasise the key importance of understanding the taxation implications before using these products.

The above is correct to the best of our knowledge and belief as at March 1996. It is, however, written as a general guide, so it is recommended that specific professional advice be sought before any action is taken.

The future

12

The way ahead

The derivatives industry is constantly changing to meet the needs of those who use it. Constant innovation, particularly in the Over-the-Counter (OTC) markets, is its life-blood – without it, it would wither and die.

Whenever a disaster, such as Barings or Sumitomo, hits the industry, it takes a long, hard look at itself, its internal controls and procedures and its safeguards against systemic risk. This has led to the unprecedented co-operation between exchanges and to widespread exchange of information. So far, a systemic breakdown has been avoided but the risk is still very real. As long as it is possible for a rogue trader to operate unchallenged, the possibilities of such a thing happening still exist. Once the rogue trader has been exposed, it is often apparent that it only required a simple, obvious and important alteration to the particular company's procedures to resolve the situation. The fact that the system has held up against all its trials and tribulations so far, is testament to its innate strength.

However, this tends to obscure the reasons for the rogue trader's existence in the first place. All too often, traders are allowed by their supervisors to operate unchecked as their explanations and assurances of even greater profits are believed. The protection of reputations – and, above all, bonuses – have caused too many supervisors, people who should know better, to turn a blind eye to their activities until it is too late and, in extreme cases, the entire company is brought to its knees. A rogue trader is not necessarily a very intelligent person – just a master of deception and someone who thinks that if he can get away with something once, he can do so again and again. If supervisors do their job properly and examine the trading on a daily basis, rogue trading will be quickly spotted and appropriate steps taken.

Market transparency

The best way of preventing a system's breakdown is to have complete openness in a market, inter-exchange co-operation and solid counterparty security. The biggest risk comes from the OTC market where many deals are tailor-made for an individual client, with the bank or investment house taking the other side. Credit ratings play a very important part in these operations. At least, where no exchanges are involved, there is less risk of a rogue trader.

The secrecy involved in many OTC deals remains a considerable cause for concern, and this is something that needs to be addressed. If the OTC market had been more open, companies like Procter and Gamble and Gibson's Greeting Cards, as well as Orange County, California, would not have found themselves in so much trouble. It is obviously very difficult to get these sorts of trades out into the open but a way will probably have to be found eventually. At present, professional jealousies and a desire to keep these operations secret from competitors are very strong and a barrier to progress.

Exchange-traded markets, on the other hand, are a different story. The desire for complete openness here is very strong and supported by most users. Co-operation between the different exchanges is a continuing process. Exchange rivalries contributed to the Barings collapse; since then, two international agreements to increase co-operation have been signed. In March 1996, over a dozen international regulators signed a declaration of co-operation and a memorandum of understanding (MOU) was signed by over 50 exchanges. Global information-sharing during crises will be strengthened and the flow of information about member firms will be speeded up between exchanges and clearing houses. The only notable absentee from the list of signatories to the MOU was Japan, whose local laws barring such agreements had first to be changed. This has now been done.

Since 1994, Marché à Terme International de France (MATIF) members have been able to trade two Deutsch Terminbörse (DTB) contracts via screens in Paris but the two exchanges have had to abandon their plans for a joint trading platform as it would require too many costly modifications to members' systems. The exchanges remain committed to a joint market for derivatives and to common clearing systems, leading to the creation of an electronic platform in Europe with a network of exchanges. Nevertheless, this serves to emphasise the difficulties involved in trying to set up any kind of joint venture.

The Futures Industry Association (FIA) has also been instrumental in ensuring more co-operation between exchanges, clearing houses, intermediaries and customers. It published a list of 60 recommendations in 1995, following the Barings crisis. This was followed by the development of a standardised information format and general instructions as a guide for participants. The format is designed to elicit information to evaluate a market's protection mechanisms, the financial resources available to cover a clearing member default and default procedures. Further information can be obtained from the FIA.

European Monetary Union (EMU)

The Capital Adequacy and Investor Services Directives (CAD and ISD), issued by the European Commission, came into force at the beginning of 1996. These have important implications for the future of the derivatives industry in the run-up to a single European currency. The removal of so many currencies from the trading books of banks and customers will leave a void to be filled, probably by non-EU currencies – although it is difficult to believe that a German Government Bond and a Greek Government Bond, both issued in Euros, will be of equal value to the market-place. Nevertheless, EMU, whether it be in 1999 or sometime later, *is* coming and the industry must be prepared for it. The future of many of the smaller European exchanges must be at risk, and many mergers are expected.

The future of Europe's derivative exchanges is likely to depend upon their relative performances and their ability to launch new contracts that prove usable by and acceptable to investors from all countries. To date, the objective of many of the smaller exchanges has been simply to create a monopoly over a stable of nationalistic contracts attractive solely to domestic investors. The advent of EMU promises to end all that and a single pan-European market is likely to cut out altogether those smaller exchanges that only have equity index contracts based on their own stock exchange.

Under the ISD, it is not necessary to have a branch office in an EU country in order to be able to trade there. However, protectionism exercised by some EU countries effectively precludes outsiders from trading on certain exchanges, and total implementation of the Directive was far from complete six months after its start date of 1 January 1996. In addition, the difficulties of reconciling different trading systems and a strong desire in some quarters to maintain the open outcry system are added drawbacks. Strict safeguards are also needed to prevent the fraudulent use of the new situation by the 'churn 'em and burn 'em' brigade of financial bandits that have appeared in the past.

Led by LIFFE, other European exchanges are exploring ways of co-operation in the run-up to EMU but it is likely that many of the smaller ones will disappear as technological advances in telecommunications lead to the diminution of the world's time zones. Already, the derivatives markets of Norway and Sweden are talking of linking up together and with Sweden's London branch, OMLX, and the two leading London exchanges, LIFFE and LCE, completed a successful merger in mid-1996.

The prospects of EMU and the subsequent disappearance of many trading currencies will cause banks to look for more opportunities in foreign exchange. The emerging market currencies of eastern Europe, Asia and Latin America are expected to benefit. These currencies are susceptible to domestic political and economic events but interest is already growing and liquidity is improving.

Many European exchanges are positioning themselves in the run-up to EMU in 1999; London, Paris and Frankfurt are all keen to have some attractive products ready for investors in good time. LIFFE and MATIF now list some of their most profitable products on the CME. By increasing business in their leading products, they are hoping to be in a dominant position when the great day arrives. Interest rate and government bond contracts denominated in the currencies of the participants will disappear on the arrival of EMU, being replaced by Euro-denominated ones; it is important therefore that the three leading financial centres are prepared for that.

CME members can now trade LIFFE's three-month Euromark futures and options products, together with MATIF's notional futures contract. This is in addition to the earlier deal between LIFFE and CBOT which allows the latter to trade LIFFE's long-term bond futures contracts and other products destined to become part of EMU.

In another move towards EMU, both LIFFE and DTB launched one-month Euromark futures in November 1996 on their respective exchanges. The main competition between these two exchanges is the trading method used on them. LIFFE is a firm believer in the open outcry method, while DTB favours the screen-based system. The relative merits of the two methods are discussed in Chapter 4.

Inter-exchange links

All the early link-ups were between exchanges in different time zones, enabling the trading hours for the most popular contracts to be extended significantly without having to go to the expense of setting up all-night trading desks. Although many exchanges have after-hours trading facilities of their own – such as LIFFE/APT, CME and MATIF/Globex, CBOT/Project A, SFE/SYCOM and NYMEX/Access – it is far easier for traders to trade the contracts on their home exchanges. Indeed, as inter-exchange links flourish, the need for these after-hours systems could disappear.

Following the very successful mutual offsetting (MOS) between CME and SIMEX which has been in operation since 1984, other exchanges are beginning to see its advantages. High-profile links, such as those between LIFFE and TIFFE, LIFFE and CBOT, NYMEX and SFE, and IPE and SIMEX, despite many false starts in the 1980s, are taking hold. Many others are at the negotiating stage and, by 1998, there should be many more of them. With the increased globalisation of futures and options trading, together with the advancing technology, such alliances make sense. They have the added advantage of forging bonds of trust between exchanges, to their mutual advantage.

The MOS between CME and SIMEX began by trading Eurodollars, the most active contract. It enabled traders to establish positions on one exchange and offset them on the other. After trading ends for the day on the CME, a trader in Chicago can execute an order on SIMEX as an extension of the Chicago market. Users of the MOS can choose between the two centres when the position will be held. In 1995, the Euroyen was added to the system.

Also in 1995, the IPE started a similar MOS with SIMEX on the former's Brent crude oil contract. Twenty-four-hour trading is also possible on the NYMEX/SFE link, which started in 1995 with NYMEX's energy futures contracts; metals were added in 1996. LIFFE and TIFFE mutually trade the Euroyen, while LIFFE similarly trades the CBOT's US Treasury bonds and the CBOT does the same with LIFFE's German bund contract. This last alliance is expected to expand quickly to include other popular contracts. Future potential links under discussion in mid-1996 included PHLX/HKFE, NYMEX/SIMEX and LIFFE/SIMEX. In September 1996, LIFFE and LCE began operating as a merged market with unified administration, exchange systems and clearing arrangements. The three leading European exchanges, LIFFE, MATIF and DTB, are positioning themselves ready to tackle the challenges ahead, up to and beyond EMU.

Although the majority of new products coming to market these days tend to be based on the screen trading method, the desire to keep open outcry trading, where it still exists, is very strong and is fiercely defended by its supporters. This is one reason why 24-hour trading systems have been slow to catch on. Inter-time zone mergers, on the other hand, can overcome this problem.

Exchange-traded versus OTC products

These mergers also encourage new products at the expense of the OTC market. OTC instruments are usually tailor-made, one-off products that do not need to travel but, where they can be adapted for use around the world, it is safer and certainly more popular to offer them via an exchange.

As stated earlier, one disadvantage of OTC instruments is their lack of transparency. They are also largely unregulated. These are causes for concern among some investors in the present climate of open and regulated exchanges. The amount of business lost to the OTC market has long been a worry to the exchanges and has led to the launching of new instruments to compete, as the latter try to take advantage of the new atmosphere and recapture some of the business.

Beginning with CME's Rolling Spot products launched in 1993, several new innovative products are now available. PHLX's United Currency Options Market (UCOM) allows trading in up to 110 currency pairs within a flexible structure – flexibility is the name of the game when it comes to competing with the OTC market. Flex options are available on CBOT, CBOE and LIFFE, where premiums, strike prices and maturity dates are negotiable.

The OTC sector itself is hoping to benefit from the expertise from exchange clearing houses in the management of the ever-rising amounts of collateral supporting the growth of the swaps business. The Chicago exchanges have responded by developing a Swaps Depository Trust (CME) and the Hybrid Instruments Transaction Service (HITS) (CBOT).

Smaller contracts

By the mid-1990s, many of the more mature futures markets were not providing the returns they once did, so investors began to pay attention to some of the smaller contracts on smaller exchanges. These showed significant growth in 1995 and 1996, with trading volumes increasing encouragingly. Rubber futures on SICOM are a case in point. There is room for expansion in developing countries. In addition, a commodity exchange in Germany is planned for 1997.

Education, regulation and clearing

For the futures and options industry to flourish in the 21st century, it is necessary to learn the lessons of the past and to improve education and training standards throughout the industry. Obsessive regulation, on the other hand, should be avoided where possible. However, the financial rewards to be gained from bending or breaking the rules are very great and too much for some trades. Both these subjects are discussed in another chapter but their importance cannot be over-emphasised. The lack of co-operation between accountancy and regulatory regimes is an obstacle that has to be overcome and harmonisation must be achieved.

An efficient, well-capitalised clearing system that crosses national boundaries will be needed for the next generation of international futures activities. Such a system could provide the key to the cross-trading between co-operating exchanges, facilitating cross-margining, trade reporting and collateral definition. The single European market created by ISD/CAD forms a trading bloc of formidable size to compete with the US and Far Eastern markets.

13

Future futures

Innovation is the key to successful derivatives trading. Whether the under-lying instrument is traded on an exchange or over the counter, a new con-tract must be liquid and volatile but, above all, it should be topical and exciting. By the mid-1990s, new contracts were being launched almost monthly, as exchanges, in particular, sought to steal a march on their rivals.

Insurance futures

Whole new families of futures contracts are emerging, as insurance, prop-erty (revised) and utilities begin to take root. Insurance futures are well established in Chicago, where six different contracts are traded, ranging from catastrophe to crop yield insurance. For some time insurance compa-nies have used the derivatives markets to hedge risks in their investment portfolios – and now they can use them to manage their other risks. An options contract is an insurance for other users but to an insurance com-pany it is, in effect, a reinsurance contract. A strong and successful market in insurance derivatives will, therefore, help increase the capacity of the reinsurance market. So far, only the CBOT lists these contracts.

The catastrophe insurance price is based on a quarterly loss-ratio index produced by the Insurance Services Office of the USA. It is calculated by dividing the total losses from catastrophes reported by 26 American insurers for a quarterly period by a premium figure that is fixed in advance. The three regional indices – eastern, mid-western and western – reflect the different risks in each area: hurricanes in the east, tornadoes and floods in the mid-west and earthquakes in the west. When Hurricane Bertha threatened America's east coast in 1996, business briefly boomed but, otherwise, business has been slow.

Over-the-Counter (OTC) business in insurance futures is considerably larger than on the CBOT, but both are growing steadily. OTC contracts are specially designed and reflect the insurer's individual spread of risks. While insurance futures are not expected to replace the reinsurance market, they will certainly complement it. The advantage of these futures is their transparency; the price of insurance policies is usually both hidden and inflexible.

The next type of insurance contract to be launched was crop yield. Modern technology can help a farmer to make all the decisions needed to prepare and grow a crop, but it is the weather that decides if a good yield comes from it. The steady scaling-back of government subsidies, in both the USA and the EU, made it essential to find a way to protect the crops. This led to the launching of a crop yield insurance contract on the CBOT, following some rather complicated reforms and inadequate and compulsory insurance schemes by the US government after the disastrous floods of 1993. The pace of agricultural reforms in the USA and EU has already led to the launching of several new wheat contracts in 1996/7.

Launched in 1995, the first crop insurance contract was based on maize yields in the main producing state of Iowa. This was followed in 1996 by a range of additional contracts covering Illinois, Indiana, Nebraska and Ohio, as well as one based on the US national average – a similar concept to the catastrophe contracts. While these contracts are aimed chiefly at end-users, fund and speculative interest should follow.

The possibilities for expansion of insurance futures contracts are endless but, so far, no other exchange has sought to follow CBOT's lead. Other insurance fields that spring to mind are motor, marine and medical.

Property futures

Another potential family of futures contracts is property. Following the ill-fated attempt by the LCE – which ended in 1991 amidst allegations that the Exchange's executives had artificially inflated trading volumes, the arguments for re-launching property contracts are very strong. Many mistakes were made at the original launching, not the least of which was the fact that no less than four contracts were listed – only one of which, UK commercial, was of any real interest to investors.

The need for commercial property to take its place on an equal footing with other financial assets is highlighted by the fact that many of the UK's largest investment institutions are advocating the launch of a property derivatives market. A range of OTC forward contracts is already available and the Real Estate Index Market (REIM) has been formed by the institutions. The REIM covers a range of contracts linked to indices produced by the Investment Property Databank (IPD), which measures the performance of £50 billion of institutionally owned UK commercial property.

A major asset class like UK commercial property needs the benefits of forward contracting. With property transaction costs being very high, a cheap derivatives market has significant advantages for the industry. So far, only commercial property is planned as there are many difficulties to be overcome before a fully-fledged property derivatives market can be formed. There are no immediate plans for any exchange-traded contracts to be listed but LIFFE is taking close interest. Once the problems have been ironed out and the commercial property index is firmly established, the possibilities for expansion will be great. The investment institutions planning to set up the market applied for authorisation from the SIB in October 1996, aiming to start operations in 1997.

New energy futures

When electricity and water futures have been successfully launched, they could take their places alongside gas futures to form a utilities futures complex allied to the energy markets. NYMEX launched an electricity futures contract at the end of March 1996 and IPE a gas one in February 1997, ushering in a new era for energy markets. Two electricity contracts were initially launched, the California–Oregon Border (COB) and the Palo Verde, Arizona contracts. At least four others soon followed. Apart from the delivery points, contract specifications of the first two are identical. Price differences between the two are largely ironed out by the differences in location, which alter peak consumption times. Peak time in the south is summer when power is needed for air conditioning; in the north it is winter for central heating. Norway also began trading electricity futures in January 1996.

New metals futures

Expansion plans for metals include aluminium in New York and Tokyo and zinc in Singapore – all set to start trading in 1997. Tokyo aluminium was launched in April. The LME's TAPO contracts will also be expanded in the next year.

New agricultural futures

Notwithstanding the vicissitudes of the weather, agricultural markets, too, are set for expansion. In 1997, CBOT financial contracts started trading in London and its agricultural ones were expected to follow quickly. The dismantling of the EU's Common Agricultural Policy (CAP), precipitated by the possibility of expanded membership to include the poorer Central European countries, should lead to more agricultural contracts being launched in Europe, following MATIF's wheat futures, launched in June 1996.

New York's CSCE launched a milk contract and a cheddar cheese one in 1993, but perishable foods cannot be stored (the milk contract is in easily stored dried milk). But technological advances in lengthening the shelf-life of fresh milk led, in December 1995 and January 1996, respectively, to the CSCE and CME launching fresh milk contracts, offering comprehensive trading opportunities in the dairy complex. Bottlers supplying schools and other large accounts and processors of ice-cream, yoghurt and other dairy products, should find these contracts particularly useful.

Other areas for expansion in agriculturals include frozen turkeys and a re-launch of the long-defunct frozen chicken and dried egg contracts. However, the apple and cranberry markets are probably too small to work successfully. The CME is aiming to launch a ground beef contract in June 1997 to complete the hamburger cycle, alongside wheat and soyabean oil, the other main ingredients.

New financial futures

The possibilities for the future of financial futures are endless. The ingenuities of market innovators know no bounds. Some of the products now available on the OTC market were considered to exist only in the realms of fantasy merely a year or so ago, and speculation as to what the future may produce is mind-boggling.

The CME formed a new division of its exchange in 1995, the Growth and Emerging Markets (GEM) division. The CBOT followed in early 1996, launching a Brady Bond complex. Both exchanges concentrated initially on Latin America which, at the time, offered the fastest growth rate among emerging countries. The possibilities for expansion into Asia and East Europe are very promising and the creation of a huge emerging markets futures complex could be imminent.

There are, already, several OTC instruments available to hedge any risk exposure to the East European equity market. Index Return Certificates offered by Bankers Trust allow access to Czech, Hungarian and Polish stock markets without having to buy the actual shares. They are based on indices for the three markets compiled by the International Finance Corporation, a branch of the World Bank.

Expansion of the sector index markets reflects the growing interest of investors. Pioneered by PHLX, nine new products were launched in the first half of 1996. Activity rose significantly and volumes rose 73% in that period. Sector index futures and options are now available on most US exchanges; they allow investors to gain exposure to a group of stocks without incurring the costs and encumbrances of buying and selling individual equities.

Conclusion

Opportunities for new contracts are endless, particularly in the financial and energy sectors; even world organisations seek to harness the derivatives markets to their own advantage. The United Nations Conference on Trade and Development (UNCTAD), while feeling that derivatives could pose a threat to developing countries, seeks to use them as risk management tools, especially in those countries with a heavy reliance on commodity exports. For instance, UNCTAD is carrying out a feasibility study for an international pepper futures contract, with KLCE as the most likely venue. A pepper futures contract was launched in India in 1997. UNCTAD wants to stabilise volatility in key commodities for the benefit of developing nations.

Much of what is written in this chapter will probably be out of date by the time this book is published, and even more exotic and unusual ideas will be the stuff of speculation. Exchanges are keen to continue to capture business from the OTC markets and this is likely to lead to all sorts of wild and wonderful ideas for new contracts in the future. So far, however, exchanges are more full of ideas than they are of actual contracts. It is time to turn these ideas into new contracts.

Contract specifications

United Kingdom

Contract	Size	Delivery months	Min fluctuation	Contract launched
Long Gilt F,OF	£50 000 NV. with 9% coupon	Mar, June, Sept, Dec	F – £1/32 = £15 625 OF – £1/64 = £7812	1982 1986
1-month Euromark IR	DM 3 million	all	0.01 = DM25	1996
3-month Euromark IR F, OF	DM 1 million	Mar, June, Sept, Dec	0.01 = DM25	F 1989 OF 1990
3-month ECU IR F	ECU $1 million	Mar, June, Sept, Dec	0.01 = ECU 25	1989
3-month Euroswiss IR F,OF	SF 1 million	Mar, June, Sept, Dec	0.01 = SF25	F 1991 OF 1992
3-month Euroyen IR F	Y100 million	Mar, June, Sept, Dec	0.01 = Y2500	1996
3-month Sterling IR F,OF	£500 000	Mar, June, Sept, Dec	0.01 = £12.50	F 1992 OF 1987
3-month Eurolira IR F,OF	ITL 1000 million	Mar, June, Sept, Dec	0.01 = ITL 25 000	F 1992 OF 1995

Contract	Size	Delivery months	Min fluctuation	Contract launched
German GB (Bund) F,OF	DM 250 000 NV + 5% coupon	Mar, June, Sept, Dec	DM 0.01 (DM25)	F 1988 OF 1989
German GB (Bobl) F, OF	DM 250 000 NV + 6% coupon	Mar, June, Sept, Dec	DM 0.01 (DM25)	1997
Japanese GB F	Y100 million	Mar, June, Sept, Dec	Y0.01 (Y10 000)	1991
Italian GB (BTP) F,OF	ITL 200 million	Mar, June, Sept, Dec	ITL 0.01 (ITL 20 000)	F 1991 OF 1991
FTSE-100 Index F	£25×index	Mar, June, Sept, Dec	0.5 (£12.50)	1984
FTSE 100 Index Option American Style	£10×index	1st 4 months + June, Dec	0.5 (£5)	1984
FTSE 100 Index Option European Style	£10×index	1st 3 months + Mar, June Sept, Dec	0.5 (£5)	1990
FTSE Mid 250 Index future	£10 + index	1st 2 months + Mar, June, Sept, Dec	0.5 (£5)	1994
Cocoa No 7	10 metric tonnes	Mar, May, July, Sept, Dec	£1 per mt	1952
Robusta coffee	5 metric tonnes	Jan, Mar, May, July, Sept, Nov	$1/t	1958
White sugar No 5[1]	50 metric tonnes	Mar, May, Aug, Oct, Dec	10c/t 5c/t (option)	1983
Potatoes	20 metric tonnes	Mar, Apr, May, June, Nov[2]	10p/t	1980
EC wheat	100 mt	Jan, Mar, May, July, Sept, Nov	5p/t	1929
EC barley	100 mt	Jan, Mar, May, Sept, Nov	5p/t	1929

APPENDIX A

Contract	Size	Delivery months	Min fluctuation	Contract launched
BIFFEX[3] Freight Index	$10 per index point	1st 3 months July, Oct	1 pt = $10	1985

[1] These contracts are traded on the Exchange's Fast Automated Screen Trading system (FAST)
[2] Options available only on April and November contracts
[3] BIFFEX = Baltic International Freight Futures Exchange

IPE

Contract	Size	Quotation	Delivery months	Min fluctuation	Contract launched
Gas Oil F,O	100 mt	$/t	F-All O – 1st 6 months	25 c/t ($25)	F – 1981 O – 1987
Brent Crude Oil F,O	1000 barrels (42000 US gallons)	$/bl	F – All O – 1st 6 months	1c/bl ($10)	F – 1988 O – 1989
Natural Gas F	1000 therms	p/therm	Negotiable[4]	0.005 p/therm	1997

[4] Delivery can be made every day throughout the year including weekends and public holidays. Contracts are for individual days, groups of days, weekly, monthly or as specified in the contract. Daily contracts cease trading at the close of business on the business day immediately prior to delivery.

LME

Contract	Quotation	Contract size	Min fluctuation
Aluminium	$/mt	25 mt	50c/t ($12.50)
Aluminium Alloy	$/mt	20 mt	50 c/t ($12.50)
Copper	$/mt	25 mt	50 c/t ($12.50)
Lead	$/mt	25 mt	50 c/t ($12.50)
Nickel	$/mt	6 mt	$1/t ($6)
Tin	$/mt	5 mt	$1/t ($5)
Zinc	$/mt	25 mt	50 c/t ($12.50)

Floor trading sessions consist of four 5-minute rings per day at the following times:

Aluminium	11.55, 12.55, 15.35 and 16.15
Aluminium Alloy	11.45, 13.05, 15.50 and 16.30
Copper	12.00, 12.30, 15.30 and 16.10
Lead	12.05, 12.45, 15.20 and 16.00
Nickel	12.15, 13.00, 15.45 and 16.25
Tin	11.50, 12.40, 15.40 and 16.20
Zinc	12.10, 12.50, 15.25 and 16.05

Open outcry (kerb) trading takes place from 13.10 to 13.30 and from 16.35 to 17.00 and the daily official prices are posted at 13.30.

Trading also takes place at other times from offices.

Options and TAPOs are also available up to 27 months ahead.

OMLX

Contract	Size	Min fluctuation	Trading months	Launched
OMX Index	SK 100× index	SK 0.01	All months	1989
Long OMX Index	SK100× index	SK 0.01	All months	O – 1992 F – 1995

The exchange also trades a range of Swedish equity futures and options.

United States

CBOT

Contract	Size	Trading months	Min fluctuation	Max fluctuation	Launch
Maize (Corn)	5000 bushels	Mar, May, July, Sept, Dec	F 1/4 c/bu ($12.50) 0 1/8 c/bu ($6.25)	12 c/bu ($600)	F–1877 O–1985
Wheat (Soft Winter)	5000 bushels	Mar, May, July, Sept, Dec	F–1/4 c/bu ($12.50) O–1.8 c.bu ($6.25)	20 c/bu ($1000)	F–1877 O–1986
Oats	5000 bushels	Mar, May, July, Sept, Dec	F–1/4 c/bu ($12.50) O–1/8 c/bu ($6.25)	10 c/bu ($500)	F–1877 O–1990

Contract	Size	Trading months	Min fluctuation	Max fluctuation	Launch
Soyabeans	5000 bushels	Jan, Mar, May, July, Aug, Sept, Nov	F 1/4 c/bu ($12.50) O 1/8 c/bu ($6.25)	30 c/bu ($1500)	F–1936 O–1984
Soyabean Meal	100 short tons	Jan, Mar, May, July, Aug, Sept, Oct, Dec	F 10 c/t ($10) O 5 c/t ($5)	$10/t ($1000)	F–1951 O–1987
Soyabean Oil	60 000 lbs	Jan, Mar, May, July, Aug, Sept, Oct, Dec	F 1/100 4/lb ($6) O 1/200 4/lb ($3)	1 c/lb ($600)	F–1950 O–1987
US Treasury Bonds	$100 000	Mar, June, Sept, Dec	F 1/32pt ($31.25) O 1/64 pt ($15.625)	3 pts ($3000)	F–1977 O–1982
10-yr US Treasury Notes	$100 000	Mar, June, Sept, Dec	F 1/32 pt ($31.25) O 1/64 pt ($15.625)	3 pts ($3000)	F–1982 O–1985
5-yr US Treasury Notes	$100 000	Mar, June, Sept, Dec	F 1/32 pt ($31.25) O 1/64 pt ($15.625)	3 pts ($3000)	F–1988 O–1990
30-day Fed Funds	$5 million	All months	0.01 ($41.67)	150 basis pts	1988
Municipal Bond Index	$1000× index	Mar, June, Sept, Dec	F–1/32 pt ($31.25) O–1/64 pt ($15.625)	3 pts ($3000)	F–1985 O–1987
Diammonium Phosphate (DAP)	100 st	1st 3 + Mar, June, Sept, Dec	10 c/t ($10)	$10/t ($1000)	1991
Anhydrous Ammonia	100 st	Feb, Apr, June, Sept, Dec	10 c/t ($10)	$10/t ($1000)	1992
Catastrophe Insurance[5]	$25000× losses/ premiums ratio	Mar, June Sept, Dec	1/10 pt ($25)	10–15 pts (variable) ($2500–3750)	1992/93

Contract	Size	Trading months	Min fluctuation	Max fluctuation	Launch
Iowa Corn Yield Insurance	Yield est × $100	Jan, Sept	1/10 bu ($10)	15 bu ($1500)	1995
Corn Yield Insurance (all states) F	Yield est × $100	Jan, Sept, Oct, Nov	1/10 bu ($10)	15 bu ($1500)	1996

ˢ There are five different catastrophe insurance contracts with identical specifications: National, Eastern, Midwestern, Western Quarterly and Western Annual. All financial products are also traded on Project A from 14.30 to 16.30 and from 22.30 to 06.30.

MIDAM

Contract	Size	Trading months	Min fluctuation	Max fluctuation	Launch
Live Cattle	20000 lbs	Feb, Apr, June, Aug, Oct, Dec	1/40 c/lb ($5)	1.5 c/lb ($300)	1978
Live Hogs	20000 lbs	Feb, Apr, June, July, Aug, Oct, Dec	1/40 c/lb ($5)	1.5 c/lb ($300)	1974
Corn (Maize)	1000 bu	Mar, May, July, Sept, Dec	1/8 c/bu ($1.25)	12 c/bu ($120)	1922
Oats	1000 bu	Mar, May, July, Sept, Dec	1/8 c/bu ($1.25)	10 c/bu ($100)	1922
Soyabeans	1000 bu	Jan, Mar, May, July Aug, Sept, Nov	1/8 c/bu ($1.25)	30 c/bu ($300)	F–1940 O–1985
Soyabean Meal	50 st	Jan, Mar, May, July, Aug, Sept, Oct, Dec	10 c/t ($5)	$10/t ($500)	1986
Soyabean Oil	30 000 lb	Jan, Mar, May, July, Aug, Sept, Oct, Dec	1/100 c/lb ($3)	1 c/lb ($300)	1995
Wheat (Soft Winter)	1000 bu	Mar, May, July, Sept, Dec	1/8 c/bu ($1.25)	20 c/bu ($200)	F–1922 O–1984

Contract	Size	Trading months	Min fluctuation	Max fluctuation	Launch
New York Gold	33.2 fine ozs	all	10 c/oz ($3.32)	None	1984
New York Silver	1000 troy ozs	all	1/10 c/oz ($1)	None	1982
Platinum	25 troy ozs	1st 3 mths +Jan, Apr, July, Oct	10 c/oz ($2.50)	$25/oz ($625)	1984
US Treasury Bonds	$50000 fv	Mar, June, Sept, Dec	F–1/32 pt ($15.62) O–1/64 pt ($7.81)	3 pts ($1500)	F–1981 O–1991
10-yr Treasury Notes	$50000 fr	Mar, June, Sept, Dec	1/32 pt ($15.62)	3 pts ($1500)	1993
Eurodollar	$500000	Mar, June, Sept, Dec	1 pt ($12.50)	None	1992
British Pound	$12500	Mar, June, Sept, Dec	0.02 c/£ ($2.50)	None	1983
Canadian Dollar	C$50000	Mar, June, Sept, Dec	0.01 c/C$ ($5)	None	1983
Deutsche Mark	DM 62500	Mar, June, Sept, Dec	0.01 c/DM ($6.25)	None	1983
Japanese Yen	JY6.25m	Mar, June, Sept, Dec	0.001 c/Y ($6.25)	None	1983
Swiss Franc	SF62500	Mar, June, Sept, Dec	0.01 c/SF ($6.25)	None	1983
Australian Dollar	A$ 50000	Mar, June, Sept, Dec	0.01 c/A$ ($5)	None	1995

CME

Contract	Size	Months	Min fluctuation	Max fluctuation	Launch
Feeder Cattle	50 000 lbs	Jan, Mar, Apr, May, Aug, Sep, Oct, Nov	2.5 c/cwt ($12.50)	1.5 c/lb ($750)	F–1971 O–1987

Contract	Size	Months	Min fluctuation	Max fluctuation	Launch
Live Cattle	40 000 lbs	Feb, Apr, June, Aug, Oct, Dec	2.5 c/cwt ($10)	1.5 c/lb ($600)	F-1964 O-1984
Lean Hogs	40 000 lbs	Feb, Apr, June, July, Aug, Oct, Dec	2.5 c/cwt ($10)	1.5 c/lb ($600)	1995
Pork Bellies	40 000 lbs	Feb, Mar, May, July, Aug	2.5 c/cwt ($10)	2 c/lb ($800)	F-1961 O-1986
Lumber (random length)	80 000 bd ft	Jan, Mar, May, July, Sept, Nov	10c/ 1000 bdft ($8)	$10/1000 bdft ($800)	1995
Grade A Milk	50 000 lbs	Feb, Apr, June, July, Sept, Nov	2.5 c/cwt ($12.50)	$2/cwt ($1000)	1996
Oriental Strand Board	100 000 ft sq	Jan, Mar, May, July, Sept, Nov	10c/MSF[6] ($10)	$10/MSF ($1000)	1996

[6] MSF 1000 sq. feet

IMM (CME)

Contract	Size	Months[7]	Min fluctuation	Max fluctuation[8]	Launch
Deutschemark	DM 125 000	Jan, Mar, Apr, June, July, Sept, Oct, Dec	0.01 c/DM ($12.50)	Variable	F-1972 O-1984
Can. Dollar	C$ 100 000	Jan, Mar, Apr, June, July, Sept, Oct, Dec	0.01 c/C$ ($10)	Variable	F-1972 O-1986
Swiss Franc	SF 125 000	Jan, Mar, Apr, June, July, Sept, Oct, Dec	0.01 c/SF ($12.50)	Variable	F-1972 O-1985

Contract	Size	Months[7]	Min fluctuation	Max fluctuation[8]	Launch
British Pound	£62 500	Jan, Mar, Apr, June, July, Sept, Oct, Dec	0.02 c/£ ($12.50)	Variable	F–1972 O–1985
Jap. Yen	JY 12.5 million	Jan, Mar, Apr, June, July, Sept, Oct, Dec	0.0001 c/Y ($12.50)	Variable	F–1972 O–1986
Aust. Dollar	A$ 100 000	Jan, Mar, Apr, June, July, Sept, Oct, Dec	0.01 c/A$ ($10)	Variable	F–1987 O–1988
French Franc	FF 500 000	Jan, Mar, Apr, June, July, Sept, Oct, Dec	0.02 c/FF ($10)	Variable	F–1993 O–1993
LIBOR[9]	$3m	All months	1 pt ($25)	None	F–1990 OF–1991
90-day Treasury Bills	$1m	Mar, June, Sept, Dec	1 pt ($25)	None	F–1976 OF–1986
Eurodollar Time Deposit	$1m	Mar, June, Sept, Dec	1 pt ($25)	None	F–1981 OF–1985
Jap. Yen Rolling Spot	$250 000	Mar, June, Sept, Dec	1 pt (Y2500)	None	1995
Deutschemark Rolling Spot	$250 000	Mar, June, Sept, Dec OF–all mths	1 pt (DM25)	None	1993
EuroYen IR	Y 100 000	Mar, June, Sept, Dec	0.01 (Y2500)	None	1996

[7] All currency contracts and the Eurodollar time Deposit contract additionally trade the spot month
[8] No daily limits during first and last 15 minutes of trading. Between those times a system of expanding limits operates.
[9] LIBOR = London Interbank Offered Rate

IOM (CME)

Contract	Size	Trading Months	Min fluctuation	Max fluctuation	Launch
Nikkei 225 Stock Average	$5× average	Mar, June, Sept, Dec	5 pts ($25)	Varies	1990

Contract	Size	Trading Months	Min fluctuation	Max fluctuation	Launch
S&P 500 Stock Index	$500× index	Mar, June, Sept, Dec	5 pts ($25)	Varies	F–1982 OF–1983
S&P Mideap 400 Index	$500× index	Mar, June, Sept, Dec	5 pts ($25)	Varies	1992
Fed Funds	$3 million	All months	1/2 pt ($12.50)	None	1996
NASDAQ 100 Index	$100× index	Mar, June Sept, Dec	5 pts ($5)	Varies	1996

NYMEX

Contract	Size	Trading Months	Min fluctuation	Max fluctuation	Launch
Heating Oil	42 000 gal	18 months forward	0.01c/gal ($4.20)	4c/gal ($1680)	F–1978 O–1987
NY Harbour Unleaded Gasoline	42 000 gal	18 months forward	0.01c/gal ($4.20)	4c/gal ($1680)	F–1984 O–1989
Crude Oil	1000 bbls (42 000 gals)	18 months forward and others up to 60 mths	1c/bbl ($10)	$1.40/bbl ($1500)	F–1983 O–1986
Natural Gas	10 000 MMB tu	First 18 months and others up to 36 months	0.1c/MMB tu ($10)	10c/MMB tu ($1000)	F–1990 O–1992
Propane Gas	42 000 gal	15 mths forward	0.01c/gal ($4.20)	4c/gal ($1680)	1987
HO/Crude Spread	1000 bbls each	1st 6 mths and 2 quarterly mths	0.01c/bbl ($10)	None	1994
Gasoline/Crude Spread	1000 bbls each	1st 6 mths and 2 quarterly mths	0.01c/bbl ($10)	None	1994
Palladium	100 troy ozs	Mar, June, Sept, Dec	5c/oz ($5)	$6/oz ($600)	1968
Platinum	50 troy ozs	Jan, Apr, July, Oct	10c/oz ($5)	$25/oz ($1250)	F–1956 O–1990

Contract	Size	Trading months	Min fluctuation	Max fluctuation	Launch
Copper	25 000 lbs	1st 12 mths + Jan, Mar, May, July, Sept, Dec[10]	1/20 c/lb ($12.50)	20 c/lb ($5000)	F–1988 O–1988
Silver	5000 ozs	1st 3 mths, + Jan, Mar, May, July, Sept, Dec[10]	F–$\frac{1}{2}$c/oz ($25) O–1/10 c/oz ($5)	$1.50 ($7500)	F–1933 O–1984
Gold	100 troy ozs	1st 3 mths + Feb, Apr, Aug, Oct[10]	10 c/oz ($10)	$75/oz ($7500)	F–1974 O–1982
Eurotop 100 Stock Index	$100× index	Mar, May, July, Dec	F–0.1pt ($10) O–0.05 pt ($5)	None	F–1992 O–1993
Electricity COB delivery[11]	736 mwh	All 18 mths fwd	1 c/mwh ($7.36)	$3/mwh ($2208)	1996
Electricity PV delivery[12]	736 mwh	All 18 mths fwd	1 c/mwh ($7.36)	$3/mwh ($2208)	1996

[10] Up to 23 months forward
[11] COB California-Oregon Border
[12] PV Palo Verde, Arizona

CSCE

Contract	Size	Trading months	Min fluctuation	Max fluctuation	Launch
Cocoa	10 metric tonnes	Mar, May, July, Sept, Dec	$1/t ($10)	$88/t ($880)	F–1925 O–1986
Coffee 'C'	37 500 lbs	Mar, May, July, Sept, Dec	F–1/20 c/lb ($18.75) O–1/100 c/lb ($3.75)	6c/lb[13] ($2250)	F–1964 O–1986
Sugar No 11	112 000 lbs	Mar, May, July, Oct	1/00 c/lb ($11.20)	$\frac{1}{2}$ c/lb[13] ($560)	F–1914 O–1982
Sugar No 14	112 000 lbs	Jan, Mar, May, July, Sept, Nov	1/00 c/lb ($11.20)	$\frac{1}{2}$ c/lb[13] ($560)	1985

Contract	Size	Trading months	Min fluctuation	Max fluctuation	Launch
Cheddar Cheese	10 500 lbs	Feb, May, July, Sept, Nov	F 1/10 c/lb ($10.50) O 1/100 c/lb ($1.05)	6 c/lb ($630)	1993
Non-fat Dry Milk	11 000 lbs	Feb, May, July, Sept, Nov	F 1/10 c/lb ($11) O 1/100 c/lb ($1.10)	6c/lb ($660)	1993
Grade A Milk	50 000 lbs	all	1 c/lb ($5)	50c ($250)	1995
White Sugar	50 MT	Mar, May, July, Oct, Dec	20 c/t ($10)	None	1996
Butter	10 000 lbs	all	1/10 c/lb ($10)	6 c ($600)	1996

[13] There are no limits on the first two quoted months

NYCE

Contract	Size	Trading months	Min fluctuation	Max fluctuation	Launch
Cotton	50 000 lbs (100 bales)	Mar, May, July, Oct, Dec	1/100 c/lb ($5)	2c/lb ($1000)	F–1870 O–1984
Frozen Concentrated Orange Juice (FCOJ)	15 000 lbs	Jan, Mar, May, July, Sept, Nov	1/20 c/lb ($7.50)	5c/lb ($750)	F–1966 O–1985
Potatoes	85 000 lbs	Jan, Mar, May, July, Sept, Nov	1 c/cwt $0.01	$2/cwt ($200)	1996

FINEX

Contract	Size	Trading months	Min fluctuation	Max fluctuation	Launch
US$/£ Exchange Rate	£62 500	Mar, June, Sept, Dec	0.01 pt ($6.25)	None	1994
US$/DM Exchange Rate	DM 125 000	Mar, June, Sept, Dec	0.01 pt ($12.50)	None	1994
US$/JY	Y12.5 m	Mar, June, Sept, Dec	0.0001 pt ($12.50)	None	1994

Contract	Size	Trading months	Min fluctuation	Max fluctuation	Launch
US$/SF	SF 125 000	Mar, June, Sept, Dec	0.01 pt ($12.50)	None	1994
Emerging Markets Debt Index (EMDX)	$1000× index	All months	0.025 pt ($25)	None	1995
US$ Index (USDX)	$1000× index	Mar, June, Sept, Dec	0.01 pt ($10)	Variable	F–1985 O–1986
2-Yr Treasury Notes	$100× basis pt of yield	All months	0.005 pt ($50)	None	1989
5-Yr Treasury Notes	$100× basis pt of yield	All months	0.005 pt ($50)	None	1987
£/DM Crossrate	£125 000	Mar, June, Sept, Dec	DM 0.001 (DM 12.50)	None	1994
DM/Yen Crossrate	DM 125 000	Mar, June, Sept, Dec	Y0.01 (Y1250)	None	1994
DM/FF Crossrate	DM 500 000	Mar, June, Sept, Dec	FF 0.0001 (FF50)	None	1994
DM/Lira Crossrate	DM 250 000	Mar, June, Sept, Dec	L0.05 (L12 500)	None	1994
DM/Krona Crossrate	DM 125 000	Mar, June, Sept, Dec	KR 0.0005 (KR 62,50)	None	1996
DM/SF Crossrate	DM 125 000	Mar, June, Sept, Dec	SF 0.0001 (SF 12.50)	None	1995

NYFE

Contract	Size	Trading months	Min fluctuation	Max fluctuation	Launch
NYSE Composite Index	$500× index	Mar, June, Sept, Dec	0.05 pt $25	18 pts ($9000)	F–1982 O–1983
CRB Futures Price Index	$500× index	Mar, May, July, Sept, Dec	0.05 pt $25	None	F–1986 O–1988

PHLX

Contract	Size	Trading months	Min fluctuation	Launch
British Pound	F–£62 500 O–£31 250	1st 2 + Mar, June, Sept, Dec	F–0.01c/£ ($6.25) O–0.01 c/£ ($3.12)	1987 1987
Deutschmark	F–DM125 000 O–DM62 500	1st 2 + Mar, June, Sept, Dec	F–0.01c/DM ($12.50) O–0.01 c/DM (6.25)	1983 1986
Swiss Franc	F–SF 125 000 O–SF 62 500	1st 2 + Mar, June, Sept, Dec	F–0.01c/SF ($12.50) O–0.01 c/SF (6.25)	1983 1986
Jap Yen	F–Y12.5m O–Y6.25m	1st 2 + Mar, June, Sept, Dec	F–0.0001c/Y ($12.50) O–0.0001c/Y ($6.25)	1983 1986
French Franc	F–FF500 000 O–FF250 000	1st 2 + Mar, June, Sept, Dec	F–0.002 c/FF ($10) O–0.002 c/FF ($5)	1984 1986
Canadian Dollar	F–C$100 000 O–C$50 000	1st 2 + Mar June, Sept, Dec	F–0.01c/C$ ($10) O–0.01c/C$ ($5)	1983 1986
Australian Dollar	F–A$100 000 O–A$50 000	1st 2 + Mar, June, Sept, Dec	F–0.01c/A$ ($10) O–0.01c/A$ ($5)	1987 1987
Spanish Peseta	O–P5 million	1st 2 + Mar, June, Sept, Dec	0.0001c/SP ($10)	1995
Italian Lira	O–L50 million	1st 2 + Mar, June, Sept, Dec	0.00001c/ITL ($10)	1995
ECU	F–125 000 O–62 500	1st 2 + Mar, June, Sept, Dec	F–0.01 c/Ecu ($12.50) O–0.01 c/Ecu ($6.25)	1986 1986
DM/Yen Exch. Rate	DM62 500	1st 2 + Mar, June, Sept, Dec	0.01 Y/DM (Y625)	1991
£/DM Exch. Rate	£31 250	1st 2 + Mar, June, Sept, Dec	0.02 DM/£ (DM6.25)	1992

KCBOT

Contract	Size	Trading months	Min fluctuation	Max fluctuation	Launch
Wheat	5000 bu	Mar, May, July, Sept, Dec	F–1/4 c/bu ($12.50) 0–1/8 c/bu ($6.25)	25c/bu ($1250)	F–1976 O–1984
Western Natural Gas	10 MMBtu	F–18 mths fwd O–12 mths fwd	1/10 c/bu ($5)	10 c/bu ($500)	1995 1995
Value Line	500× index	Mar, June, Sept, Dec	0.05 pt ($25)	Variable	1982
Mini Value Line	100× index	Mar, June, Sept, Dec	0.05 pt ($5)	Variable	F–1983 O–1992

MGE

Contract	Size	Trading months	Min fluctuation	Max fluctuation	Launch
Wheat (Hard Red Spring)	5000 bu	Mar, May, July, Sept, Dec	F–1/4c/bu $12.50 O–1/8 c/bu ($6.25) ($1000)	20 c/bu ($1000)	F–1893 O–1984
Wheat (white)	5000 bu	Mar, May, July, Sept, Dec	F–1/4c/bu $12.50 O–1/8 c/bu ($6.25) ($1000)	20 c/bu ($1000)	F–1984 O–1991
White Shrimp	5000 lbs	Mar, June, Sept, Dec	F–1/4c/bu $12.50 O–1/8 c/bu ($6.25) ($1000)	20 c/bu ($1000)	F–1993 O–1993
Black Tiger Shrimp	5000 lbs	Mar, June, Sept, Dec	F–1/4c/bu ($12.50) O–1/8 c/bu ($6.25) ($1000)	20 c/bu ($1000)	F–1994 O–1994
Barley	180 000 lbs	Mar, May, July, Sept, Dec	1/2 c/lb ($9)	25 c/lb ($450)	F–1996 O–1996

France

MATIF

Contract	Size	Trading months	Min fluctuation	Launch
Long-Term Notional Bond	FF500 000	Mar, June, Sept, Dec	F–0.02 % (FF100) O–0.01 % (FF50)	1986 1988
3-month Pibor[14]	FF5 m	Mar, June, Sept, Dec	F–0.01 % (FF125) O–0.005 % (FF62.5)	1988 1990
Ecu Bond	Ecu100 000	Mar, June, Sept, Dec	0.02 % (Ecu20)	1990
CAC 40 Stock Index	FF200× index	1st 3 mths + Mar, June, Sept, Dec	0.5pt (FF100)	1988
White Sugar	50 mt (bagged)	Mar, May, Aug, Oct, Dec	10 c/t (US$5)	1964
Rapeseed	50 mt	Feb, May, Aug, Nov	DM 1/t (DM50)	1995
Wheat	50 mt	Feb, May, Sept, Nov	FF 1/mt (FF50)	1996
DM/FF Exch. Rate[15]	DM100 000	1st 3 + Mar, June, Sept, Dec	0.01 % (DM10)	1995
US$/FF Exch. Rate[15]	$100 000	1st 3 + Mar, June, Sept, Dec[16]	0.01 % ($10)	1994
US$/DM Crossrate[15]	$100 000	1st 3 + Mar, June, Sept, Dec[16]	0.01 % ($10)	1994
£/DM Crossrate[15]	DM100 000	1st 3 + Mar, June, Sept, Dec[16]	0.01 % (£5)	1995
DM/Lira Crossrate[15]	DM100 000	1st 3 + Mar, June, Sept, Dec[16]	0.01 % (DM10)	1995

MONEP[15]

Contract	Size	Trading months	Min fluctuation	Launch
CAC40 Stock Index	FF200× index	1st 2 mths + Mar, June, Sept, Dec	FF0.01/pt (FF2)	1988
Long-Term CAC 40 SI	FF50× index	Mar, Sept, two years fwd	FF0.01/pt (FF0.5)	1991

Options on a range of equities also traded.

[14] PIBOR = Paris Interbank Offered Rate
[15] Options only
[16] Additionally, one fortnightly position is traded

Germany

DTB

Contract	Size	Trading months	Min fluctuation	Launch
Long-Term Government Bond (Bund)	DM250 000 (6% Coupon)	Mar, June, Sept, Dec	0.01pt (DM25)	F–1990 O–1991
Medium-Term GB (Bobl)	DM250 000 (6% Coupon)	Mar, June, Sept, Dec	0.01pt (DM25)	F–1991 O–1993
German Stock Index (DAX)	F,OF DM100 × Ix O DM 10 × Ix	1st 3 mths + Mar, May, Sept, Dec[17]	F–0.5 pt (DM50) O–0.1pt (DM1) OF–0.1pt (DM10)	1990 1991 1992
FIBOR[18]	DM 1m	1st 3 mths + Mar, May, Sept, Dec[17]	0.01% (DM25)	1994
1m EuroDM IR	DM 3m	all	0.01 (DM25)	1996
3 m EuroDM IR	DM 1m	all	0.01 (DM25)	1997

Australia

SFE

Contract	Size	Trading months	Min fluctuation	Launch
90-day Bank Bills[19]	A$1m FV	Mar, June, Sept, Dec	0.01% (A$24)	F–1979 OF–1985
All -Ordinaries Share Price Index[19]	A$25× index	Mar, June, Sept, Dec	1 pt (A$25)	F–1983 OF–1985
3-Yr Treasury Bonds[19]	A$100 000 (12% coupon)	Mar, June, Sept, Dec	0.01 pt (A$28)	F–1984 OF–1985
10-Yr Treasury Bonds[19]	A$100 000 (12% coupon)	Mar, June, Sept, Dec	0.005% (A$37)	F–1984 OF–1985
Wool	2500 kg	Feb, Apr, June, Aug, Oct, Dec	1 c/kg (A$25)	1995
Wheat	50 MT			1996

A range of equity futures contracts are also traded on the SFE.

[17] Only 9 months forward
[18] Frankfurt Interbank Offered Rate
[19] These contracts are also traded on SYCOM, the exchange's overnight screen training system.

Austria

OTOB

Contract	Size	Trading months	Min fluctuation	Launch
Austrian Traded Index	Ast100 × index	1st 3 months + last mth of next quarter	Ast 0.10 (Ast 10)	F,O–1992
Austrian Government Bonds	Ast 1m	Mar, June, Sept, Dec	0.01% (Ast 100)	F–1993

Equity Options, Long-term equity options and East European equity indices are also traded

Belgium

BELFOX

Contract	Size	Trading months	Min fluctuation	Launch
Belgian Government Bonds	BF2.5m (9% coupon)	Mar, June, Sept, Dec	0.01pt (BF250)	F–1993 OF–1994
3-month BIBOR[20]	BF25m	Mar, June, Sept, Dec	0.01pt (BF625)	F–1994
BEL20 Equity Index	F–BF1000 × index O–BF100 × index	All months	F–0.1pt (BF100) O–0.1pt (BF10)	F–1992 O–1993
Gold Index	BF100 × index	All months	BF1	O–1995
US$/BF Exchange Rate	US$10 000	Mar, June, Sept, Dec	0.01pt (BF100)	O–1994

[20] Brussels Interbank Offered Rate. Equity options also traded.

Brazil

BM&F

Contract	Size	Trading months	Min fluctuation	Launch
IBOVESPA Stock Index	BR0.20 × index	Feb, Apr, June, Aug, Oct, Dec	F–50 pt(BR10) OF–1pt (BR0.20)	1986 1994
1-Day Interbank Deposits	BR50 000	All months	F–BR0.05 OF–BR0.005	1991 1994
30-Day Interbank Deposits	BR50 000	All months	BR0.05	F–1991
US Dollar (Commercial)	$10 000	All months	BR0.001/$1000 (BR0.01)	F–1987 O–1991
US Dollar (Floating)	$10 000	All months	BR0.001/$1000 (BR0.01)	F–1991 O–1991
C Bond[21]	$100 000 FV	All months		F–1996

Contract	Size	Trading months	Min fluctuation	Launch
Gold	250 grams	All months	BR0.001/gr (BR0.25)	F–1986 O–1986
Gold	1 kg	All months	0.1c/gr ($1)	F–1993
Coffee Arabica	100 bags of 60 kg	Mar, May, July, Sept, Dec	0.1c/bag ($1)	F–1989 OF–1991
Coffee Robusta	100 bags of 60 kg	Jan, Mar, May, July, Sept, Nov	5 c/bag ($5)	F–1992
Live Cattle	330 Arrobas[22]	All months	1 c/steer ($3.30)	F–1991 OF–1994
Feeder Cattle	33 140-kg steers	All months	1 c/steer ($3.30)	F–1992
Cotton	12 750 kg	Mar, Apr, May, July, Oct, Dec	1 c/lb ($281)	F–1991
Soyabeans	27 metric tonnes	Mar, May, July, Sep, Nov	1 c/60 kg ($4.50)	F–1995
Crystal Sugar	270 50-kg bags	Mar, May, Aug, Oct, Nov	1 c/60 kg ($4.50)	F–1995

[21] Capitalisation bond
[22] 1 arroba = 15 kg

Canada

MONTREAL EXCHANGE

Contract	Size	Trading months	Min fluctuation	Max fluctuation	Launch
3-Month Canadian Bankers A[23]	C$ 1 m FV	F–Mar, June, Sept, Dec O–1st 4 mths	0.01 % (C$25)	None	F–1988 O–1994
10-Yr Canadian GB	C$ 100 000	Mar, June, Sept, Dec	0.01 % (C$10)	3 pts (C$3000)	F–1989 O–1991
5-Yr Canadian GB	C$ 100 000 (NV, 9 % coupon)	Mar, June, Sept, Dec	0.01 % (C$10)	3 pts (C$3000)	F–1995

Contract	Size	Trading months	Min fluctuation	Max fluctuation	Launch
Canadian GB	C$25 000	1st 3 mths + 2 quarterlies	0.01% (C$2.50)	None	O–1982

Equity options on 27 stocks and LEAP options on 10 stocks are also traded.
[23] A – Acceptance

Toronto Stock Exchange

Contract	Size	Trading months	Min fluctuation	Launch
TSE100 Stock Index	100 × index	1st 2 mths + 2 Quarterlies	Varies[24]	1994
TSE 35 Stock Index	100 × index	1st 2 mths + 2 Quarterlies	Varies[24]	1987

Exchange also trades stock and leap options plus participation units on the above stock indices – details from the exchange.

[24] Under C10c, C1c,
C10c – C$5, C5c,
over C$5, C12.5c

Winnipeg Commodity Exchange (WCE)

Contract	Size	Trading months	Min fluctuation	Max fluctuation	Launch
Canola	20 & 100 metric tonnes[25]	Jan, Mar, June, Aug, Sep, Oct	100 c/t (C$2 & 10)	C$10/t (C$200 & 1000)	F–1963 O–1991
Flaxseed	20 & 100 metric tonnes[25]	Mar, May, July, Oct, Dec	100 c/t (C$2 & 10)	C$10/t (C$200 & 1000)	F–1904 O–1993
Oats	20 & 100 metric tonnes[25]	Mar, May, July, Oct, Dec	100 c/t (C$2 & 10)	C$5/t (C$100 & 500)	F–1904 O–1993
Domestic Feed Wheat	20 & 100 metric tonnes[25]	Mar, May, July, Oct Dec	100 c/t (C$2 & 10)	C$5/t (C$100 & 500)	F–1974 O–1992
Domestic Feed Peas	20 & 100 metric tonnes[25]	Feb, May, July, Oct, Dec	100 c/t (C$2 & 10)	C$5/t (C$100 & 500)	F–1995

Contract	Size	Trading months	Min fluctuation	Max fluctuation	Launch
Western Domestic Feed Barley	20 mt	Feb, May, Aug, Nov	C10c/t (C$2)	C$5/t (C$100)	F–1989 O–1993

[25] Trading can be in either 20-tonne job lots or 100-tonne board lots.

China

Beijing Commodity Exchange[26]

Contract	Size	Trading months	Min fluctuation	Max fluctation
Corn (Maize)	10 mt	Jan, Mar, May	1 year/t (10 y)	40 y
Plywood	400 pieces	All months	2y/100p (4 y)	150 y
Copper	5 MT	All months	10 y/t (50 y)	2%
Peanuts	10 MT	Jan, Mar, May, July, Sept, Nov	2 y/t (20 y)	150 y
Green Beans	10 MT	Jan, Mar, May, July, Sept, Nov	2 y/t (20 y)	120 y
Polypropylene	10 MT	All months	5 y/t (50 y)	250 y
Sodium Carbonate	10 MT	All months	2 y/t (20 y)	60 y
Rubber	10 MT	Feb, Apr, Jun Aug, Oct, Dec	10 y/t (25 y)	400 y

[26] Futures only

Denmark

FUTOP

Contract	Size	Trading months	Min fluctuation	Launch
Danish GB 2006	DK 1m	Mar, Jun, Sept, Dec	0.02 (DK200)	F–1994 OF–1994
Danish GB 2001	DK 1m	Mar, June, Sept, Dec	0.02 (DK200)	F 0 1992 OF–1992

Contract	Size	Trading months	Min fluctuation	Launch
Mortgage Credit Bonds	DK 1m (6 % coupon)	Mar, June, Sept, Dec	0.02 (DK200)	F–1993
KFX Stock Index	DK 1 m	All months	0.05 (DK 50)	F–1989 O–1989
3-month CIBOR[27]	DK 5m	Mar, June, Sept, Dec	0.01 (DK125)	F–1993

[27] CIBOR = Copenhagen Interbank Offered Rate

Finland

Finnish Option Exchange

Contract	Size	Trading months	Min fluctuation	Launch
NBSK pulp	50 tonnes	all	$1	1997

Hong Kong

HKFE

Contract	Size	Trading months	Min fluctuation	Launch
Hang Seng Stock Index	HK$50 × index	1st 3 mths + Feb, Apr, June, Aug, Oct, Dec	1 point(HK$50)	F–1986 O–1993

Currency and equity futures also traded.

Hungary

Budapest Commodity Exchange

(Futures Only)

Contract	Size	Trading months	Min fluctuation	Launch
Corn (Maize)	20 MT	Mar, May, July, Oct, Nov, Dec	HF 10/t (HF8000)	1989
Milling Wheat	20 MT	Jan, Mar, May, July, Aug, Sept, Oct, Dec	HF 10/t (HF8000)	1989
Feed Wheat	20 MT	Jan, Mar, May, July, Aug, Sept, Oct, Dec	HF 10/t (HF8000)	1989
Feed Barley	20 MT	Jan, Mar, May, July, Aug, Sept, Oct, Dec	HF 10/t (HF8000)	1989
Black Seed	20 MT	Mar, May, Sept, Oct, Dec	HF 10/t (HF8000)	1989
Deutschmark	DM1 000	Mar, June, Sept, Dec	HF0.01/DM (HF2000)	1993
US Dollar	$1000	Mar, June, Sept, Dec	HF0.01/$ (HF 3000)	1993
Jap Yen	Y100 000	Mar, June, Sept, Dec	HF0.01/Y100 (HF3000)	1994
British Pound	£1000	Mar, June, Sept, Dec	HF0.01/£(3000)	1996
Italian Lira	L/ra	Mar, June, Sept, Dec	0.01/1000L (3000)	1996
Swiss Franc	SF 1000	Mar, June, Sept, Dec	0.01/SF (3000)	1996
ECU	1000	Mar, June, Sept, Dec	0.01/ECU (3000)	1996

Not all contracts are traded every week day.

Italy

Italian Stock Exchange

Contract	Size	Trading months	Min fluctuation	Launch
MIB 30 Stock Index	F–L100m O–L10 000/pt	Mar, June, Sept, Dec	F–5 points O–1 point	1994 1995

Equity options were introduced in 1996.

Japan

TOCOM
(Futures Only)

Contract	Size	Trading months	Min fluctuation	Launch
Gold	1 kg	Spot month + even months	Y1/gr (Y1000)	1982
Silver	60 kg	Spot month + even months	Y0.1/10 gr (Y3000)	1984
Platinum	500 g	Spot month + even months	Y1/gr (Y500)	1984
Palladium	1.5 kg	Spot month + even months	Y1/gr (Y1500)	1992
Rubber	5000 kg	1st 6 months	Y0.1/kg (Y500)	1952
Cotton Yarn	1814.36 kg	1st 6 months	Y0.1/lb (Y400)	1951
Wool	500 kg	1st 6 months	Y1/kg (Y500)	1953

An aluminium contract was launched in 1997.

TGE

Contract	Size	Trading months	Min fluctuation	Launch
US Soyabeans	30 000 kg	Feb, Apr, Jun, Aug, Oct, Dec	Y10/1000kg (Y3000)	F–1984 O–1991

Contract	Size	Trading months	Min fluctuation	Launch
Red Beans (Azuki)	80 bags (2400 kg)	1st 6 months	Y10/bag (Y800)	F–1952
Corn (Maize)	100 000 kg	Jan, Mar, May, July, Sept, Nov	Y10/1000 kg (Y10 000)	F–1992
Refined Sugar	9000 kg	1st 6 months	Y0.1/kg (Y900)	F–1952
Raw Sugar	50 000 kg	Jan, Mar, May, July, Sept, Nov	Y10/1000 kg (Y5000)	F–1952 O–1992

TIFFE

Contract	Size	Trading months	Min fluctuation	Launch
3-month Euroyen	Y100m	Mar, June, Sept, Nov	0.01pt (Y10 000)	F–1989 OF–1991
3-month Eurodollar	US$1m	Mar, June, Sept, Nov	0.01 pt ($25)	F–1989
1-year Euroyen	Y100m	Mar, June, Sept, Nov	0.01 pt (Y10 000)	F–1992
$/Yen Exchange Rate	$50 000	Mar, June, Sept, Nov	0.05 c/Yen (Y2500)	F–1990

TSE

Contract	Size	Trading months	Min fluctuation	Launch
10-Yr Jap GB	Y100m	Mar, June, Sept, Nov	0.01 pt (Y10 000)	F–1985 OF–1990
20-Yr Jap GB	Y100m	Mar, June, Sept, Nov	0.01 pt (Y10 000)	F–1988
US T-Bonds	$100 000	Mar, June, Sept, Nov	1/32 pt = $31.25	F – 1989
Tokyo Stock Index (TOPIX)	Y10 000×index	Mar, June, Sept, Nov[28]	F–1 pt (Y10 000) O–1/2pt (Y5 000)	1988 1989
5-Yr Jap GB	Y100m	Mar, June, Sept, Dec	0.01 pt (Y10 000)	1996

[28] Options are traded all months

KANEX

Contract	Size	Trading months	Min fluctuation	Launch
Azuki Beans	2400 kg	1st 6 mths	Y10/30 kg (Y800)	F–1952
Soyabeans (Imported)	30 MT	Feb, Apr, June, Aug, Oct, Dec	Y 10/t (Y300)	F–1976
Raw Sugar	50 MT	Jan, Mar, May, July, Sept, Nov	Y10/t (Y500)	F–1952 O–1991

KRE

Contract	Size	Trading months	Min fluctuation	Launch
Natural Rubber	5000 kg	1st 6 months	Y0.1/kg (Y500)	F–1952

OSE

Contract	Size	Trading months	Min fluctuation	Launch
Nikkei 225 Stock Index	Y1000 × index	Mar, June, Sept, Dec	Y10/pt (Y10 000)	F–1988 O–1989
Nikkei 300 Stock Index	Y10 000 × index	Mar, June, Sept, Dec	0.1pt (Y1000)	F–1994 O–1994

Malaysia

KLCE

Contract	Size	Trading months	Min fluctuation	Launch
Crude Palm Oil	25 MT	1st 6 mths then alternate	M$1/t (M$25)	1980

Cocoa, rubber and tin contracts are also extant but tradeless.

KLOFFE

Contract	Size	Trading months	Min fluctuation	Launch
KLSE Composite Index (CI)	C1 × RM100	1st 2 + 2 Quarterlies	0.1pt (RM10)	1996

Netherlands

EOE – Optiebeurs

Contract	Size	Trading months	Min fluctuation	Launch
EOE Stock Index	F–FL200 × index O–FL100 × index	1st 3 months + Jan, Apr, July, Oct	F–FL0.05 O–FL0.10 (FL100)	1987 1987
Top Five Index	F–FL200 × index O–FL100 × index	1st 3 months + Jan, Apr, July, Oct	FL0.10 (F–FL200 O–FL100)	F–1990 O–1990
Eurotop 100 Index	Ecu50 × index	1st 3 mths + Mar, June, Sept, Dec	Ecu 0.10 (Ecu 5)	F–1991 O–1991
Government Bonds[29]	FL10 000 NV	Feb, May, Aug, Nov	FL0.01 (FL100)	O–1994

[29] FLEX options also available. Equity options on 42 Dutch stocks are also traded.

ATA

Contract	Size	Trading months	Min fluctuation	Launch
Wheat	125 MT	Feb, Apr, Jun, Aug, Oct, Dec	DM 0.25/t (DM 31.25)	1996
Potatoes	25 000 kg	Feb, Mar, Apr, May, Jun, Nov	DFL 0.10/100 kg (FL25)	1958
Live Pigs	10 000 kg (app. 100 pigs)	All months	DFL 0.005/kg (FL50)	1980
Piglets	100 piglets of 23 kg each	All months	DFL 0.25/kg	1991

New Zealand

NZ FOE

Contract	Size	Trading months	Min fluctuation	Launch
90-day Acceptance Bills	NZ$500 000	Mar, June, Sept, Dec	0.01 % (NZ$5)	F–1986 OF–1986
3-Yr Government Stock	NZ$100 000	Mar, June, Sept, Dec	0.01pt (NZ$1)	F–1993 OF–1993
10-Yr Government Stock	NZ$100 000	Mar, June, Sept, Dec	0.01pt (NZ$1)	F–1991 OF–1991

Philippines

MIFE
(Futures Only)

Contract	Size	Trading months	Min fluctuation	Launch
Sugar	112 000 lbs	1st 6 months	2c/lb (= $2240)	1986
Soyabeans	500 60 kg bags	1st 6 months	50 c/kg (= $2500)	1986
Copra	20 000 kg	1st 6 months	1 c/kg (= $200)	1988
Coffee	5000 kg	1st 6 months	5 c/kg (= $100)	1988
Dry Cocoon	300 kg	1st 6 months	50 c/kg ($150)	1992
$/Yen	Y12.5m	1st 4 months	Y0.01	1991
$/DM	DM125 000	1st 4 months	DM0.0001	1991
$/SF	SF125 000	1st 4 months	SF0.0001	1991
£/$	$1100 000	1st 4 months	$0.0001	1991

Trading was suspended on this exchange in mid-1996.

Singapore

SIMEX

Contract	Size	Trading months	Min fluctuation	Launch
Euroyen	Y100m	Mar, June, Sept, Dec	0.01pt (Y2500)	F 1989 OF 1989
Eurodollar	$1m	Mar, June, Sept, Dec	0.01pt ($25)	F 1984 OF 1984
Japanese GB	Y50m (10-Yr 6% coupon)	Mar, June, Sept, Dec	Y0.01 (Y5000)	F 1993 OF 1993
Nikkei 225	Y500 × average	Mar, June, Sept, Dec	5 pts (Y2500)	F 1986 OF 1986
Nikkei 300	Y10 000 × futures price	Mar, June, Sept, Dec	0.1 pt (Y1000)	F–1995 OF–1995
$/Yen Deferred Spot	$100 000	Mar, June, Sept, Dec	Y0.01/$ (Y1000)	F 1993
$/DM Deferred Spot	$100 000	Mar, June, Sept, Dec	DM0.0001/$ (DM10)	F 1993
Fuel Oil	100 MT	1st 9 months	10 c/t ($10)	F 1989
Brent Crude Oil	1000 bbl	1st 12 months	1 c/bbl ($10)	F 1995

South Africa

SAFEX

Contract	Size	Trading months	Min fluctuation	Launch
All-Share Index	R10 × index	Mar, June, Sept, Dec	1 pt	F,O 1987
Gold Index	R10 × index	Mar, June, Sept, Dec	1 pt	F,O 1987
JSE Ind-Index	R10 × index	Mar, June, Sept, Dec	1 pt	F,O 1987

Spain

MEFF-RF

Contract	Size	Trading months	Min fluctuation	Launch
90-day MIBOR[30]	SP100m	1st 8 months	1pt (SP2500)	F,OF 1995
360-day MIBOR	SP100m	1st 8 months	1pt (SP10 000)	F,OF 1995
10-Yr GB	SP10m	Mar, June, Sept, Dec	1pt (SP1000)	F 1992 OF 1992
German Diff	SP10m	Mar, June, Sept, Dec	1 pt (SP1000)	1996
French Diff	SP10m	Mar, June, Sept, Dec	1 pt (SP1000)	1996
Italian Diff	SP10m	Mar, June, Sept, Dec	1 pt (SP1000)	1996

[30] MIBOR = Madrid Interbank Offered Rate

MEFF-RV

Contract	Size	Trading months	Min fluctuation	Launch
IBEX-35 Stock Index	SP1000 × index	All months	1pt (SP100)	F 1992 O 1992

Plus Options on equities

Sweden

OMS

Contract	Size	Trading months	Min fluctuation	Launch
OMX Stock Index	SK100 × index	All months	SK 0.01	F 1987 O 1988
180-day T-Bills	SK1 m	Mar, June, Sept, Dec	0.01 pt	F 1992
2-Yr T-Bonds	SK1 m	Mar, June, Sept, Dec	0.01 pt	F 1992
5-Yr T-Bonds	SK1 m	Mar, June, Sept, Dec	0.01 pt	F 1990 O 1994
10-Yr T-Bonds	SK1 m	Mar, June, Sept, Dec	0.01 pt	F 1990

Switzerland

SOFFEX

Contract	Size	Trading months	Min fluctuation	Launch
Swiss Market Index	F 50 × index O 5 × index	1st 3 mths + Jan, Apr, July, Oct	F 0.1pt (SF5) O varies	1990 1988
Swiss GB	SF100 000	Mar, June, Sept, Dec	0.01% (SF10)	F 1992 O 1994

Also Equity options on 14 stocks.

B

Exchange addresses

Agrarische Termijnmarkt Amsterdam bv
Damrak 261, Postbus 529 1000, Netherlands
Tel: 31-20-638-2258
Fax: 31-20-626-5459

Austrian Futures and Options Exchange
Strauchgasse 1-3, P O Box 192, A-1014 Vienna, Austria
Tel: 43-1-531-65-0
Fax: 43-1-532-97-40

Beijing Commodity Exchange
306 Chonyun Building, 8 Beichen East Road, Chaoyang District, Beijing, 100101 China
Tel: 86-1-492-8347
Fax: 86-1-493-3183

Belgian Futures and Options Exchange
Palais de la Bourse, Rue Henry Maus, 2, 1000 Brussels, Belgium
Tel: 32-2-512-80-40
Fax: 32-2-513-83-42

Bolsa de Mercadorias and Futuros
The Commodities and Futures Exchange
Praea Antonio Prado, 48, Sao Paulo SP 01010-901, Brazil
Tel: 55-11-232-5454
Fax: 55-11-232-7565

Budapest Commodity Exchange
H-1373, P O Box 495, H-1134, Budapest, Hungary
Tel: 36-1-269-8571
Fax: 36-1-269-8575

Chicago Board Options Exchange
400 S. LaSalle Street, Chicago, IL 60605, USA
Tel: 1-312-786-5600
Fax: 1-312-786-7409

Chicago Board of Trade
141 W Jackson Boulevard, Chicago,
IL 60604-2994, USA
Tel: 1-312-435-3500
Fax: 1-312-341-3306

Chicago Mercantile Exchange
30 S. Wacker Drive, Chicago, IL
60606, USA
Tel: 1-312-930-1000
Fax: 1-312-930-3439

**Coffee, Sugar and Cocoa
Exchange Inc**
4 World Trade Center, New York,
NY 10048, USA
Tel: 1-212-742-6100
Fax: 1-212-748-4321

Danish FUTOP Market
Copenhagen Stock Exchange,
Nikolaj Plads 6, Box 1040, DK-
1007, Copenhagen, Denmark
Tel: 45-33-93-3366
Fax: 45-33-12-8613

Deutsche Terminbörse
60284 Frankfurt, Boersenplatz 7-11,
Germany
Tel: 49-69-2101-0
Fax: 49-69-2101-2005

European Options Exchange
Rokin 65, 1012 KK, Amsterdam,
Netherlands
Tel: 31-20-550-4550
Fax: 31-20-623-0012

Hong Kong Futures Exchange
5/F Asia Pacific Finance Tower,
Citibank Plaza, 3 Garden Road,
Hong Kong
Tel: 852-842-9333

Fax: 852-810-5089

**International Petroleum
Exchange**
International House, St Katherine's
Way, London E1 9UN, UK
Tel: 44-171-481-0643
Fax: 44-171-481-8485

**Irish Futures & Options
Exchange**
Segrave House, Earlsfort Terrace,
Dublin 2, Ireland
Tel: 353-1-676-7413
Fax: 353-1-661-4645

Italian Stock Exchange
Piazza degli Affarib, 20123, Milan,
Italy
Tel: 39-2-72-42-61
Fax: 39-2-72-00-43-33

**Kansai Agricultural
Commodities Exchange**
1-10-14 Awaza, Nishi-ku, Osaka
550, Japan
Tel: 81-6-531-7931
Fax:81-6-541-9343

Kansas City Board of Trade
4800 Main Street, Suite 303, Kansas
City, MO 64112, USA
Tel: 1-816-753-7500
Fax: 1-816-753-3944

Kobe Rubber Exchange
5-28 Kyutaro-Machi 2-Chome,
Chou-ku, Osaka 541, Japan
Tel: 81-6-244-2191
Fax: 81-6-243-4427

Kuala Lumpur Commodity Exchange
4th Floor Citypoint, Komplex
Dayabumi, Jalan Sultan
Hishamuddin, P O Box 11260,
50740 Kuala Lumpur, Malaysia
Tel: 60-3-293-6822
Fax: 60-3-274-2215

Kuala Lumpur Options and Financial Futures Exchange BHD
10th Floor, Exchange Square, Off
Jalan Semantea Damawara Heights,
50490, Kuala Lumpur, Malaysia
Tel: 60-3-253-8199
Fax: 60-3-253-5911

London Bullion Market Association
6 Frederick's Place, London EC2R
8BT, UK
Tel: 44-171-796-3067
Fax: 44-171-796-4345

London Commodity Exchange
1 Commodity Quay, St Katherine's
Dock, London E1 9AX, UK
Tel: 44-171-481-2080
Fax: 44-171-702-9923

London International Financial Futures Exchange
Cannonbridge, London EC4R 3XX,
UK
Tel: 44-171-623-0444
Fax: 44-171-588-3624

London Metal Exchange
56 Leadenhall Street, London EC3A
2BJ, UK
Tel: 44-171-264-5555
Fax: 44-171-680-0505

Manila International Futures Exchange
7/F First Bank Centre, Paseo de
Roxas, Makati 1200, The
Philippines
Tel: 63-2-818-5496
Fax: 63-2-818-5529

Marché a Terme International de France
115 Rue Reaumur, 75002, Paris,
France
Tel: 33-1-40-28-82-82
Fax: 33-1-40-28-80-01

Marché de Options Negociable de Paris
SCMC 39 Rue Cambon, 75001,
Paris, France
Tel: 33-1-49-27-18-00
Fax: 33-1-49-27-18-23

Meff Renta Fija
Via Laietana 58, 08003 Barcelona,
Spain
Tel: 34-3-412-1128
Fax: 34-3-268-4769

Meff Renta Variable
Torre Picasso, Planta 26, 28020,
Madrid, Spain
Tel: 34-1-585-0800
Fax: 34-1-571-9542

Minneapolis Grain Exchange
400 S. Fourth Street, Minneapolis,
MN 55415, USA
Tel: 1-612-338-6212
Fax: 1-612-339-1155

Montreal Exchange
Stock Exchange Tower, P O Box 61,
800 Victoria Square, Montreal,

Quebec H42 1A9, Canada
Tel: 1-514-871-2424
Fax: 1-514-871-3531

New York Cotton Exchange
4 World Trade Center, New York,
NY 10048, USA
Tel: 1-212-742-5050
Fax: 1-212-748-1241

New York Mercantile Exchange
4 World Trade Center, New York,
NY 10048, USA
Tel: 1-212-758-3000
Fax: 1-212-842-5263

New Zealand Futures and Options Exchange
P O Box 6734, Wellesley Street,
10th Level, Stock Exchange Centre,
Auckland, New Zealand
Tel: 64-9-309-8308
Fax: 64-9-309-8817

OM Stockholm AB
Brunkebergstorg 2, Box 16305,
S103 26 Stockholm, Sweden
Tel: 46-8-700-0600
Fax: 46-8-723-1092

OMLX, The London Securities and Derivatives Exchange
107 Cannon Street, London EC4N
5AD, USA
Tel: 44-171-283-0678
Fax: 44-171-815-8508

Osaka Securities Exchange
8-16 Kitahama, 1-Chome, Chou-ku,
Osaka 541, Japan
Tel: 81-6-229-8643
Fax: 81-6-231-2639

Oslo Stock Exchange
P O Box 460, Sentrum, N-0105,
Oslo, Norway
Tel: 47-22-34-17-00
Fax: 47-22-41-65-90

Philadelphia Stock Exchange
1900 Market Street, Philadelphia,
PA 19103, USA
Tel: 1-215-496-5000
Fax: 1-215-496-5653

Singapore Commodity Exchange
111 North Bridge Road, 23-04/05,
Peninsular Plaza, Singapore 0617
Tel: 65-338-5600
Fax: 65-338-9116

Singapore International Monetary Exchange
1 Raffles Place N007-00 OUB
Centre, Singapore 048616
Tel: 65-535-7382
Fax: 65-535-7282

South African Futures Exchange
105 Central Street, Houghton Estate
2198, P O Box 4406, Johannesburg
2000, RSA
Tel: 27-11-728-5960
Fax: 27-11-728-5970

Swiss Options and Financial Futures Exchange
Selnaustrasse 32, CH-8021, Zurich,
Switzerland
Tel: 41-1-229-2111
Fax: 41-1-229-2233

Sydney Futures Exchange
30-32 Grosvenor Street, Sydney,
NSW 2000, Australia
Tel: 61-2-256-0555

Fax: 61-2-256-0666

Tokyo Commodity Exchange
10-8 Nihonbashi Horidomeeho, 1-
Chome, Chou-ku, Tokyo 103, Japan
Tel: 81-3-3661-9191
Fax: 81-3-3661-7568

Tokyo Grain Exchange
12-5 Nihonbashi-Kakigera-Cho,
1-Chome, Chou-ku, Tokyo 103,
Japan
Tel: 81-3-3668-9321
Fax: 81-3-3661-4564

**Tokyo International Financial
Futures Exchange**
1-3-1 Marunouchi, Chiyoda-ku,
Tokyo 100, Japan
Tel: 81-3-5223-2400
Fax: 81-3-5223-2450

Tokyo Stock Exchange
2-1 Nihombashi-Kabuto-Cho,
Chou-ku, Tokyo 103, Japan
Tel: 81-3-3666-0141
Fax: 81-3-3663-0625

Toronto Stock Exchange
2 Frist Canadian Place, The
Exchange Tower, Toronto, Ontario,
M5X 1J2, Canada
Tel: 1-416-947-4700
Fax: 1-416-947-4662

Winnipeg Commodity Exchange
500 Commodity Exchange Tower,
360 Main St, Winnipeg, Manitoba
R3C 324, Canada
Tel: 1-204-925-5000
Fax: 1-204-943-5448

Other useful addresses

Futures Industry Association
2001 Pennsylvania Avenue NW,
Suite 600, Washington DC 20006-
1807, USA
Tel: 1-202-466-5460
Fax: 1-202-296-3184

**The Futures and Options
Association**
Aldgate House, 33 Aldgate High
Street, London EC3N 1EA, UK
Tel: 44-171-426-7250
Fax: 44-171-426-7251

**Securities and Futures
Authority**
Cottons Centre, Cottons Lane,
London SE1 2QB, UK
Tel: 44-171-378-9000
Fax: 44-171-403-7569

**Securities and Investments
Board**
Gavrelle House, 2-14 Bunhill Row,
London EC1Y 8RA, UK
Tel: 44-171-638-1240

C

Glossary of terms

Actuals: Physical commodities which underline futures contracts.

Against actuals: See Exchange for physicals.

Arbitrage: The simultaneous purchase and sale of a commodity or financial instrument in different markets to take advantage of a price or exchange rate discrepancy.

Asset allocation: The distribution of funds in different markets for diversification purposes.

Back months: A futures contract where the maturity is beyond the spot month.

Backwardation: The price differential between spot and back months when the nearby dates are at a premium. The opposite of a contango.

Bar chart: A chart that plots the high, low and closing prices by means of a vertical line between the first two and a bar to indicate the closing price.

Base metals: Metals that lose their metallic lustre and easily tarnish at ordinary temperatures, that is all non-precious metals.

Basis price: See Strike price.

Bear: An investor who believes prices will decline.

Benchmark: A reference index which serves as a basis for performance comparisons.

Borrowing (LME):   Buying a nearby date on the LME and simultaneously selling a date further forward.

Bretton Woods: The currency agreement of 1944 which fixed exchange rates for major currencies and the price of gold at $35 per ounce. It was rescinded in 1972.

Bucket shop: A derogatory term for an unregulated investment house.

Bull: An investor who believes prices will rise.

Butterfly spread: The placing of two inter-delivery spreads in opposite directions with the centre delivery month common to both. The perfect butterfly would require no net premium payment.

Call option: An option that gives the buyer the right to buy a futures contract, at a premium, at the strike price.

Cash settlement: The settlement of a futures contract in cash as opposed to delivery of the underlying instrument.

Charting: See Technical analysis

Churning: Trading for the sake of generating commission rather than in the interests of the client.

Clearing house: An agency or company that is responsible for settling trades, collecting margins, regulating delivery and reporting trading data. It acts as the principal to all contracts.

Commission house: See Futures commission merchant.

Commodity Credit Corporation: A branch of the US Department of Agriculture that supervises the government's farm loan and subsidy programmes.

Commodity futures trading commission (CFTC):   A federal regulatory agency that oversees all futures trading in the USA.

Commodity pool: A fund contributed by a number of investors for trading futures and options at a bigger level than would otherwise be possible.

Commodity swap: A swap in which counterparties exchange cash flows based on commodity prices on at least one side.

Contango: The price differential between spot and back months when the marking dates are at a discount. The opposite of backwardation.

Corner: Possession of sufficient tonnage of a commodity to be able to dictate prices and terms to other members, to their disadvantage. Nowadays, markets have safeguards to prevent such a thing happening.

Crack spread: Trading crude oil against gasoline or other refined products. An oil refiner's operating margin.

Crush spread: Trading soyabeans against soyabean oil and/or meal. A soyabean processor's operating margin.

Currency swap: A swap in which the counterparties exchange equal amounts of two currencies at the spot exchange rate.

Daily trading limit: The maximum price range as laid down by the exchange authorities.

Day trade: A transaction completed within a day.

Declaration: The agreed date and time by which the purchaser of an option must state his intention to exercise or abandon it. Failure to do so is construed as abandoning the option.

Delivery month: The month in which the futures contract matures and within which delivery, if appropriate, is made.

Delta: The change in option price for a given change in the price of the underlying. The probability that the underlying will move in-the-money by expiration.

Deposit: Money or other collateral left with a licensed deposit taker, to earn a return. Also, the initial outlay demanded by a broker in order to trade futures and options.

Derivative: A financial product whose value in whole or in part is determined directly or indirectly by reference to the price of an underlying security.

Double option: An option that gives the buyer the right to buy and/or sell a futures contract, at a premium, at the strike price. Such premiums are normally twice the level of calls or puts.

Eurocurrency: Any currency that is outside the formal control of the issuing countries' monetary authorities. The prefix describes only the geographical origins of the currency. Soon we shall have the Euroeuro.

Exchange for physicals: A transaction used by two hedgers who wish to exchange futures for spot positions to take or make delivery of the underlying commodity. Also known as Against actuals.

Exercise of an option: The purchase or sale of a call or put option by the holder of the option, at the strike price.

Exercise price: See Strike price.

Exotic option: Any of a wide variety of options with unusual underlyings or conditions. Available on the OTC market, they are often tailor-made for individual clients. Also known as Non-standard options.

Expiration date: The final settlement date of a futures or options contract.

Face value: The value of a bond at maturity or a notional principal amount.

Fex Alliance: The First European Exchange Alliance which was set up in 1992 between OM, OMLX, EOE-Optiebeurs, SOFFEX and OTOB.

First notice day: The first day, under the rules of the relevant exchange, on which notices of intentions to deliver actual commodities against futures market positions can be made or received.

Force majeure: The clause in a physical contract which allows the seller not to deliver due to reasons outside his control, such as natural disasters, strikes, acts of God, etc. There is no such clause in a futures contract.

Frontrunning: The illegal practice of trading before executing an order on the market with the intention of obtaining a financial advantage.

Fundamental analysis: A method of forecasting future price movements using supply and demand and other factual information.

Fungibility: The standardisation and interchangeability of futures and options contracts. Not all financial contracts are necessarily fungible, despite having identical terms.

Futures & Options Funds (FOFs):   Unit trusts that are able to make use of derivative instruments.

Futures Commission Merchant (FCM):   A broker or company that solicits and executes orders in a futures market. Also referred to as Commission Houses or Wine Houses.

Futures contract: A legally binding agreement for the purchase and sale of a commodity, index or financial instrument some time in the future.

Globalisation: The trend towards looking at economic and financial issues, etc, from a worldwide rather than a single country viewpoint.

Globex: An electronic exchange for trading around the clock. Other such exchanges are Access, Project A and LIFFE'S ATS.

Hedge, hedging: The practice of offsetting an equal but opposite position in the futures market.

Hedge fund: A large pool of private money and assets managed aggressively and often riskily on any futures exchange, mostly for short-term gain. In spite of the name, these funds are not engaged in hedging in any form – just the opposite.

Index: A number calculated by weighting a number of prices or rates according to a set of predetermined rules to form a benchmark for that sector or market.

Index fund: A fund designed to track the performance of a market or sector index.

Initial margin: The deposit required by an investor to trade in futures markets. Usually set by the exchanges.

Instrike: The trigger or barrier price at which an in option becomes a conventional one.

In-the-money option: An option with intrinsic value. A call option is in-the-money if its strike price is below the current price of the underlying futures contract and a put option is in-the-money if it is above the underlying.

Kerb trading: Trading outside ring dealing times on the LME. Originally this was done outside the exchange itself on the side of the street but is now done via the telephone.

Last trading day: The day on which trading ceases for a particular delivery month or period.

Lending (LME):   Selling a nearby date on the LME and simultaneously buying a date further forward.

Leverage: The ability to control large positions in a futures market with a comparatively small amount of capital.

LIBOR: London Interbank Offered Rate – the standard international reference for interest rates.

Lifting a leg: Closing out one side of a straddle or other risk-offsetting exercise in the hope of increasing profit on the open side.

Liquidity: A market condition where sufficient volume allows large transactions to be traded without having a significant impact on price stability.

Long: Starting a trade by purchasing futures contracts.

Lot: The minimum unit of contract for a particular commodity.

Managed futures: A pool or fund of futures contracts owned by more than one person and run by a manager.

Margin call: A demand from a clearing house to a clearing member or from a broker to a customer to bring deposits up to a required minimum level to guarantee performance at ruling prices.

Mark to market: A process of valuing an open position on a futures market against the ruling price of the contract at that time, in order to determine the size (if any) of the margin call.

Momentum indicators: See Oscillators.

Moving average: An average of the last 5, 10, 20 or some other number of days plotted on a chart in conjunction with the closing price. The crossing of these two lines is the signal to trade.

Mutual offset: A system whereby a position in one market can be offset against one in another by arrangement between exchanges.

Naked option: An option granted without any offsetting physical or cash instrument for protection. Such activity can lead to unlimited losses.

Nearby month: The first quoted month of a futures contract. Also called the spot month.

Netting agreements: The contractual offsetting of positions in a market.

Non-standard options: See Exotic option.

Notionnel: The French Government bond contract traded on MATIF.

Off-exchange: See Over-the-counter.

Open interest: The total number of futures or options contracts not offset by an opposite position.

Open outcry: A method of trading that entails buyers and sellers to shout their wares loud enough for all other participants to hear.

Open position: A forward or futures position which has not been closed out.

Option: A contract that, for a premium, conveys the right but not the obligation to buy or sell a futures position for a limited period at an agreed price, known as the strike price.

Oscillators: Indicators that measure the speed at which a price is moving. Many of them are designed to oscillate between 0 and 100. They are most efficient in a sideways market.

Out-of-the-money option: An option with no intrinsic value. A call option is out-of-the-money if its strike price is above the underlying and a put option is so if it is below the underlying.

Over-the-counter (OTC): An instrument that is not traded on a conventional exchange. Such instruments are often tailor-made for individual customers and can be created with any provisions allowed by law. Such markets are unregulated, so counterparty risk is an important consideration.

Pari passu: Two securities or obligations that have equal rights to payment.

Payment-in-kind (PIK): A US government programme in which farmers who comply with a voluntary acreage-control programme and set aside an additional percentage of specified acreage, receive certificates that can be redeemed for government owned stocks of grain.

Performance bond: Another name for deposits and margin.

Physicals: See Actuals.

Pit: The trading area where futures and options are bought and sold by open outcry.

Plain vanilla: A standard financial option with no strings attached.

Premium (options): The price of an option. The non-returnable sum of money paid to the grantor.

Put option: An option that gives the buyer the right to sell a futures contract, at a premium, at the strike price.

Pyramiding: The practice of using excess margin from a successful speculative operation to increase the size of the open position.

Relative strength indicator (RSI): A graph that measures the price of a contract against an appropriate yardstick or benchmark.

Ring: The official trading on the LME.

Risk disclosure statement: A document enumerating the risks involved in trading futures and options. It must be signed by all partcipants.

Rocket scientist: The media's description of a creator of risk management products. Sometimes used as a deprecatory remark.

Secondary market: The traditional exchange or OTC market when previously issued instruments are traded.

Securities and Futures Authority (SFA): The regulatory body in charge of the securities and derivatives markets in the United Kingdom.

Securities and Investment Board: The regulatory body in charge of all financial markets of the United Kingdom. It overseas the SFA.

Securitisation: Future flow transactions involving any source of hard currency exports including commodity exports, telephone and credit card receivables and cross-burden electricity supply that can be used to boost the credit ratings of emerging market countries.

Settlement: The process in which a trade is enticed on to the books of the participants.

Settlement price: The price fixed for the internal settlement of futures contracts at maturity.

Short: Starting a trade by selling a futures contract.

Spread: The difference between the bid and asked prices in any market.

Spot month: The first deliverable month for which a quotation is available on a futures market.

Squeeze: Pressure on a particular delivery that distorts its price against other deliveries.

Stochastic process: A mechanism for describing future prices or rates based on a combination of prices or rates and a random variable.

Stop-loss orders: An order placed in the market to buy or sell to close out an open position in order to limit losses when the market moves the wrong way.

Straddle: The simultaneous purchase and sale of the same commodity in different delivery months or different exchanges.

Strangle: A similar operation to a straddle, but involving options. Sometimes known as a surf and turf.

Strike price: The price at which the futures contract underlying an option can be traded. Also referred to as exercise price.

Surf and turf: See Strangle.

Swap: An agreement to exchange one currency or index return for another, the exchange of fixed interest payments for floating rate payments or the exchange of an equity index return for a floating interest rate.

Switching: Transferring an open position into a later delivery period. Sometimes referred to as rolling forward.

Systemic risk: Risk associated with the possibility of a total collapse of the entire financial system in the world.

Technical analysis: The practice of forecasting future price movements from past ones plotted on to a graph and interpreted according to a preconceived pattern or put theory.

Tender: Delivery against a futures contract.

Texas hedge: A transaction that increases risk.

Tick or tick size: The minimum price fluctuation allowed by the rules of the exchange.

Triple witching hour: The trip congruence of stock option, index option and index futures expirations on the third Friday of March, June, September and December which led to brief flurries of extra-ordinary trading activity and greatly enhanced volatility. Much to the disappointment of the media, a series of changes to market structure and the broader dissemination of information have largely diffused this situation.

Underlying: The currency, commodity, security or other instrument that forms the basis of a futures or options contract.

Value date: The date on which the parties to a currency or swap transaction settle their obligations.

Variation margin: The cash required to bring an open futures position to the current market level at the end of each working day.

Volatility: A measurement of the change in price over a given time frame. Often expressed as a percentage, it is the annualised standard deviation of percentage change in the daily price.

Volume: The number of purchases or sales of a futures contract made each day.

Warrant (LME): The document of title to a metal in a registered warehouse.

Whipsaw: A sharp price movement quickly followed by a sharp reversal.

Wirehouse: See Futures Commission Merchant.

Writer: A grantor (seller) of options.

D

Abbreviations

Throughout this book, the various exchanges are referred to by their short initials, etc. These are as follows:

BELFOX	Belgian Futures and Options Exchange
BM&F	Bolsa de Mercadorias & Futuros (Brazil)
CBOE	Chicago Board Options Exchange
CBOT	Chicago Board of Trade
CME	Chicago Mercantile Exchange
COMEX	Commodity Exchange (Division of NYMEX)
CSCE	Coffee, Sugar and Cocoa Exchange (New York)
DTB	Deutsche Terminbörse (Germany)
EOE-Optiebeurs	European Options Exchange (Netherlands)
FINEX	Financial Exchange (Division of NYCE)
FUTOP	Copenhagen Stock Exchange (Denmark)
GEM	Growth and Emerging Markets Exchange (Division of CME)
HKFE	Hong Kong Futures Exchange
IFOX	Irish Futures and Options Exchange
IMM	International Monetary Market (Division of CME)
IOM	Index and Options Market (Division of CME)
IPE	International Petroleum Exchange (London)
KCBOT	Kansas City Board of Trade
KLCE	Kuala Lumpur Commodity Exchange

KLOFFE	Kuala Lumpur Options and Financial Futures Exchange
LBMA	London Bullion Market Association
LCE	London Commodity Exchange
LIFFE	London International Financial Futures Exchange
LME	London Metal Exchange
MATIF	Marché à Terme International de France
MEFF-RF	Meff Renta Fija (Spain)
MEFF-RV	Meff Renta Variable (Spain)
MGE	Minneapolis Grain Exchange
MIDAM	Mid America Commodity Exchange (Chicago)
MIF	Italian Stock Exchange
MIFE	Manila International Futures Exchange
MONEP	Marché des Options Negociable de Paris
NYCE	New York Cotton Exchange
NYFE	New York Futures Exchange (Division of NYCE)
NYMEX	New York Mercantile Exchange
NZFOE	New Zealand Futures and Options Exchange
OM	OM Stockholm (Sweden)
OMLX	The London Securities and Derivatives Exchange
OSE	Osaka Securities Exchange (Japan)
OTOB	Austrian Futures and Options Exchange
PHLX	Philadelphia Stock Exchange
SAFEX	South African Futures Exchange
SFE	Sydney Futures Exchange (Australia)
SICOM	Singapore Commodity Exchange
SIMEX	Singapore International Monetary Exchange
SOFFEX	Swiss Options and Financial Futures Exchange
TGE	Tokyo Grain Exchange
TIFFE	Tokyo International Financial Futures Exchange
TOCOM	Tokyo Commodity Exchange
TSE	Tokyo Stock Exchange
WCE	Winnipeg Commodity Exchange (Canada)

Other abbreviations in the book are as follows:

AA	Against Actuals
BIS	Bank for International Settlements
CAD	Capital Adequacy Directive
CFTC	Commodity Futures Trading Commission (US)
CPO	Commodity Pool Operator
CTA	Commodity Trading Adviser
DFM	Derivative Fund Manager
EFP	Exchange for Physicals
EMU	European Monetary Union

EU	European Union
FCM	Futures Commission Merchant
FOA	Futures and Options Association
FSA	Financial Services Act
FX	Foreign Exchange
HTA	Hedged to Arrive
IRS	Interest Rate Swaps
ISD	Investor Services Directive
MASP	Monthly Average Settlement Price
MOS	Mutual Offset
MOU	Memorandum of Understanding
MTM	Mark(ed)-to-Market
OEICS	Open Ended Investment Companies
OTC	Over-the-Counter
SEC	Securities Exchange Commission (US)
SFA	Securities and Futures Authority
SIB	Securities and Investments Board
SRO	Self Regulatory Organisation
TAPOS	Traded Average Price Options
VAR	Value at Risk

E

Some exotic options

All-or Nothing Option: An option with a fixed, predetermined payoff if the underlying instrument is at or beyond the strike at expiration. Also called a Digital Option.

Asian Option: See Average Rate Option

Atlantic Option: See Bermuda Option

Average Rate Option: An option whose settlement value is based on the difference between the strike and the average price of the underlying on selected dates over its life, or over a period beginning on some start date and ending at expiration. Also called an Asian Option because they were invented in Japan.

Barrier Option: Path-dependent options with both their payoff pattern and their survival to the nominal expiration date not only on the final price of the underlying but on whether or not the underlying sells at or through a barrier price during the life of the option. Also called a Trigger Option.

Basket Option: A third party option or covered warrant on a basket of underlying stocks, currencies or commodities.

Bermuda Option: Like the location of Bermuda, this option is located somewhere between a European-style option which can be exercised only at maturity and an American-style option which can be exercised any time the option holder chooses.

Bull-cum-Bear Option: A zero coupon note made up of a deep in-the-money call and a deep in-the-money put, either of which can be closed out prior to maturity to convert the overall position to either a call or a put.

Capped Index Options (CAPS): An exchange-traded, single contract, vertical option spread with European-style exercise plus an early exercise price trigger. CAPS incorporate in a single contract either two index calls or two index puts with the same expiration date and with strike prices 30 points apart. The two options are traded as a single, inseparable option spread contract.

Combination Option: An option containing at least one put and one call. The component options may be exercised or re-sold separately but they are originally traded as a unit.

Compound Option: An option on an option, such as a put on a call, a call on a put, a call on a call or a put on a put.

Constant Maturity Treasury Option: A contract in which the buyer of the option pays no premium up front but agrees to pay a pre-determined premium if the option has *any* value at expiration. (See Deferred Premium Option.)

Cross-Currency Option: An outperformance option struck at an exchange rate between two currencies.

Cross-Rate Options: Currency options on two currencies that are not standard in the market where options are traded.

Currency Swap Option: An option to buy or sell a currency swap at a specific exchange rate.

Deferred Premium Option: An option without an upfront premium. At expiration, the premium is paid or netted against any option payoff.

Deferred Strike Price Option: An option that permits the buyer of the contract to set the strike price at a fixed ratio to the spot price at any time during an interval following the date of the trade. Unless the buyer sets the strike price earlier, it is determined by the spot price at the end of the deferred start period.

Double Barrier Option: An option that has two instrikes, outstrikes or trigger prices (See Barrier Options)

Down-and-In Option: A contract that becomes a standard call option if the underlying drops to the instrike price.

Down-and-Out Option: A call option that expires if the market price of the underlying drops below a pre-determined outstrike price.

Dual Currency Option: An option which settles in either of two currencies at the choice of the option holder.

Embedded Option: An option that is an inseparable part of another instrument. Most are conversion features granted to the buyer or early termination options granted to the issuer of a security by the buyer.

Fraption: An option on a forward rate agreement. (Also known as an Interest Rate Guarantee).

Hindsight Currency Option: An option giving the buyer the retroactive right to buy a currency at its low point (the call) or to sell it at its high point (the put), within the option period.

Interest Rate Option: A right but not an obligation to pay or receive a specific interest rate on a pre-determined principal for a set period.

Knock-in and Knock-out Options: Types of Barrier Options.

Ladder Option: An option that provides an upward reset of its minimum payout when the underlying touches or trades through certain price levels or attains a certain level on designated reset dates. Also called a Lock-Step Option.
Lock-Step Option: See Ladder Option.
Lookback Option: An option giving the buyer the retroactive right to trade the underlying at its minimum or maximum within the lookback period.
Lookforward Option: An option giving the buyer the prospective right to the difference between the strike price and its high (call) or low (put) over the period.

Multi-Index Option: An outperformance option with a payoff determined by the difference in performance of two or more indices.

Outperformance Option: An option with a payoff based on the amount by which one of two underlying instruments or indices outperforms the other. (Also known as Margrabe, Multi-Index and Relative Performance Options.)
Over-The-Top Option: Any option that changes the rate of participation in a rate or price movement beyond the strike (also known as a profit-sharing option).

Plain Vanilla Option: A straightforward option with no frills or gimmicks whatsoever.
Pop-up Option: See Up-and-In Option.

Quantity Adjusting Option (Quantos): (A) A fixed exchange rate foreign equity option in which the face amount of the currency coverage expands or contracts to cover changes in the foreign currency value of a designated underlying security or package of securities. (B) An option on a percentage change in a currency pair ratio applied to a face amount denominated in a third currency.

Rainbow Option: See Outperformance Option.
Ratchet Option: See Ladder Option.
Reduced Cost Option: Any option with a reduced premium resulting from the sale of another option or acceptance of a less favourable strike price.
Relative Performance Option: See Outperformance Option.

Secondary Currency Option: An option with a payoff in a different currency than the underlying's trading currency.
Swaption: An option to enter into a swap contract.
Switchback Option: A complex instrument combining a capped call and an up-an-in put or a floored put and a down-and-in call.

Tandem Options: A sequence of options of the same type, usually covering non-overlapping time periods and often with variable strikes.
Touch Option: Any of several variations of barrier options which become in, out or explode in an early exercise trigger when the instrike, outstrike or early exercise price is touched a certain number of times.
Trigger Option: See Barrier Options.

Up-and-Away Option: See Up-and-Out Option
Up-and-In Option: See Barrier Option.
Up-and-Out Option: The call pays off early if an early exercise price trigger is hit. The put expires worthless if the market price of the underlying risks above a pre-determined expiration price.

Vanishing Option: An option with an expiration price, such as a down-and-out call or an up-and-out put.

Weighted Average Rate Option: Similar to the average rate option except that the weighting of each daily, weekly or monthly price or rate varies depending on the agreement of the parties.

Zero Strike Price Option: An option with an exercise price of zero, or close to zero, traded on exchanges where there is a transfer tax, owner restriction or other obstacle to the transfer of the underlying.

Index

American Exchange of New York, 27

Baltic Futures Exchange, 16
Bank of England, 22, 94, 111
Bankers Trust, 96
Barings Bank, 7, 82, 93, 96, 101
Barratz, Dr Morton, 74
Basle Committee for Banking
    Supervision, 103
Boca Raton, 8
Bretton Woods, 14, 26
Butter and Cheese Exchange, 27

Cannonbridge, 14
Chicago Produce Exchange, 25
China International Trust &
    Investment Corporation, 98
Citrus Associates, 29
Coldelco, Corporation, Chile, 96
Coffee Exchange of New York, 28
Commodity Futures Trading
    Commission (CFTC), 98, 114, 115
crack spread, 46
crush spread, 46

Daiwa Corporation, 96
Donchian, Richard, 70
Dow, Charles, 83

Elliott, R N, 83
European Community, 18, 104
European Managed Futures
    Association, 74
European Parliament, 104

Fibonacci, Leonardo, 83
First European Exchanges Alliance, 23
First World War, 5
Financial Services Act, 21, 22, 49, 51,
    106
Futures and Options Association, 117,
    122
Futures Industry Association, 101, 139

Gann, William D, 84
Garroway's Coffee House, 3
George, Eddie, 112
Gibson Greetings Cards, 96, 138
Gold Exchange of Singapore, 37
Great Tulip Crash, the, 94
Greenspan, Alan, 111
Gruber, Martin J, 74

Hedge Funds, 7
HM Treasury, 111
Hong Kong Commodity Exchange, 38

IBM, 64
Inland Revenue, 124
International Coffee Agreement, 88
International Organisation of Securities
    Commissions (IOSCO), 103
International Tin Council, 20, 95
Investment Property Databank, 146
Investors Compensation Scheme, 109
Irwin, Dr Scott, 74

Keynes, John Maynard, 70

Leeson, Nick, 7, 36, 45
LHW, 96
Lintner, Professor, 73
London Clearing House, 17, 107
London Commercial Salerooms, 3
London Daily Price, 18
London Gold Fix, 23

Markowitz, Dr Harry, 73
Metallgeschellschaft, 96, 97
Mackay, Charles, 94

National Futures Association, 114
neural networks, 13

Orange County, California, 82, 96, 97,
    138
Organisation of Petroleum Exporting
    Countries, 88

Orr, Alma, 74

Proctor and Gamble, 138
Prudential-Bache, 96

Real Estate Index Market (REIM), 146
Rentzler, Gerald C, 74
ring dealing times, 20
Royal Exchange, 3

Salomon Brothers, 96
Schneiweiss, Dr Tom, 74
Schwager, Jack, 74
Securities and Exchanges Commission,
    114
Securities and Futures Authority, 115,
    117, 118, 119
Securities and Investments Board, 105,
    146
South Sea Company, 94
SPAN, 19, 38
Stock Exchange, the, 52
Sumitomo Corporation, 22, 96
Sydney Greasy Wool Exchange, 34

TED spread, 46

UNCTAD, 148

World Bank, 64, 148